LEARNING
TO WALK WITH GOD LIKE
ENOCH

EMMANUEL S. OMERE

WESTBOW
PRESS®
A DIVISION OF THOMAS NELSON
& ZONDERVAN

This book is a work of non-fiction. Unless otherwise noted, the author and the publisher make no explicit guarantees as to the accuracy of the information contained in this book and in some cases, names of people and places have been altered to protect their privacy.

WestBow Press books may be ordered through booksellers or by contacting:

WestBow Press
A Division of Thomas Nelson & Zondervan
1663 Liberty Drive
Bloomington, IN 47403
www.westbowpress.com
844-714-3454

Because of the dynamic nature of the Internet, any web addresses or links contained in this book may have changed since publication and may no longer be valid. The views expressed in this work are solely those of the author and do not necessarily reflect the views of the publisher, and the publisher hereby disclaims any responsibility for them.

Any people depicted in stock imagery provided by Getty Images are models, and such images are being used for illustrative purposes only. Certain stock imagery © Getty Images.

Scripture quotations marked KJV are taken from the Holy Bible, King James Version.

Scripture quotations marked NKJV are taken from the New King James Version. Copyright © 1982 by Thomas Nelson, Inc. Used by permission. All rights reserved.

ISBN: 979-8-3850-2064-5 (sc)
ISBN: 979-8-3850-2065-2 (e)

Library of Congress Control Number: 2024904446

Print information available on the last page.

WestBow Press rev. date: 02/28/2024

TABLE OF CONTENT

DEDICATION

This book is dedicated to the Almighty and everlasting Father, the Lord, the Creator of the ends of the earth, Who fainteth not, neither is He weary and there is no searching of His understanding. He is the One Who giveth power to the faint; and to people like my humble self who have no might or power, He gives us power and He increases our strength so that we can overcome all the physical and spiritual battles from Satan and his evil forces launched against us as well as all challenges of life. May His name be glorified forever in Jesus name

ACKNOWLEDGEMENT

I want to acknowledge the support of my wife Mrs. Faith Omere my children and all my friends in Nigeria and in the United States of America, who have been very supportive of my ministry and my call into the service of my creator the Almighty God.

I also want to express my deep appreciation to my senior pastors, Pastor Abiodun David (RO) MFM Boston, Pastor Bamidele Omotosho and Pastor Precious Omolade (RO) MFM Region 109, Ikotun Lagos. Who has been of immense spiritual support to me and my family. Thank you so much.

I also want to express my gratitude to MFM Boston members such as Elder George Obichie (the great encourager), Mama Georgia Okoye, Prof & Mrs Banwo, Wole Ademola just to mention a few.

And to my wonderful brother Imuetinyan Omere, your labor of love cannot be forgotten thank you so much. I also want to thank the Director of Omere International Evangelical & Soul Winning Ministries, Pastor Wilson Adegite.

God bless you all.

PREFACE

God's desire for every child of His is an intimate relationship. Our Creator loves to relate to us every day in all matters as we trudge along the dark alleyways of life, holding our hands firmly in His big hand. The essence of a walk with God is the divine guidance we get from Him from time to time, helping us in the process to align ourselves with His perfect will for us. The goal is to achieve the purpose of why we were sent to the planet Earth on a tour of duty. If we are to achieve our existential purposes, then we need daily divine counsel, instructions, guidance, and direction for the journey of life from God. When we walk with Him, our thoughts, desires, utterances, and deeds will be pleasing to God. But walking with God is not just a walk in the park. It comes with some challenges, especially for the end-time generations.

Nevertheless, these challenges are not insurmountable. We can overcome them by drawing inspiration from the experiences of great men and women of faith in the Bible who walked with God successfully. Among these people were Enoch and Noah. They were human beings like us; they weren't perfect or sinless, yet the Bible declared in the Book of Genesis 5 verse 24 that **"And Enoch walked with God: and he was not;"** and in Genesis 6 verse 9 that **"Noah was a just man and perfect in his generations, and Noah walked with God. (see** Genesis 5:24 and in Genesis 6 verse 9 KJV**)**

In his letter to Christians in the City of Corinth and its environs, Apostle Paul declared: **Now all these things happened unto them for ensamples: and they are written for our**

XI

admonition, upon whom the ends of the world are come.." (1Corinthians 10:11 KJV)** Thus, the records of the wonderful deeds of the great men and women of faith, especially Enoch, who walked with God successfully, are meant to be sources of great inspiration for us as we, too, take the steps to walk with God. We can make a success of our walk with God by learning from Enoch and other people like him, emulating what made them so successful and exceptional in their personal and active relationship with God. Walking with God requires obedience, faithfulness, and righteousness. It is to completely abstain from the world and its ways of life, as the Apostle James told us in James 4:4 that friendship with the world is enmity with God.

Walking with God entails shunning the seat of the scornful, as the Psalmist puts it. Psalm 1:1. "**Blessed is the man that walketh not in the counsel of the ungodly, nor standeth in the way of sinners, nor sitteth in the seat of the scornful. (Psalm 1:1, KJV).** To walk with God is to avoid evil and do well, as Apostle Peter declared in 1 Peter 3:11–12.

**"Let him eschew evil, and
do good; let him seek peace,
and ensue it. For the eyes of the
Lord are over the righteous, and his
ears are open unto their prayers: but the
face of the Lord is against them that do
evil. (Peter 3:11-12. Peter 3:11-12. KJV)**

A man or woman who walks with the Lord is a person of faith who consciously decides to devote himself or herself to a daily walk with God and live a godly, faith-filled life pleasing to Him, irrespective of the daily challenges of life, our daily concerns, hopes, dreams, and struggles. Enoch and Noah pleased God with their absolute and constant faith in him. They had loving, trusting, and humble spirits and lived for God every day, doing His will. Dear reader, if you want to have a successful walk with the Lord like these patriarchs, then you must cultivate the same attributes they had and also exhibit them in your everyday life.

Indeed, the longer we walk closely with God, the better we will know him. He will continually open our eyes to His will. His Spirit in us will reveal His wisdom and purpose to us. In the words of Apostle Paul, in the book of Colossians, it is declared thus:

For this cause, we also, since the day we heard it, do not cease to pray for you, and to desire that ye might be filled with the knowledge of his will in all wisdom and spiritual understanding; That ye might walk worthy of the Lord unto all pleasing, being fruitful in every good work, and increasing in the knowledge of God; strengthened with all might, according to his glorious power, unto all patience and longsuffering with joyfulness; (Colossians 1:9–11 KJV)

Apostle Paul further counselled all those who want to walk with God in Chapter 2 of the Colossians:

As ye have therefore received Christ Jesus the Lord, so walk ye in him: Rooted and built up in

him, and stablished in the faith, as ye have been taught, abounding therein with thanksgiving. (Colossians 2:6-7 KJV)

As we make up our minds to walk side-by-side with God in the journey of life I pray that the Lord will give us the grace and power to have a successful walk with Him like Enoch and Noah. Amen.

Emmanuel S. Omere

CHAPTER ONE

GOD DESIRES A PERSONAL RELATIONSHIP WITH YOU

Many years ago, when I was growing up in Benin City, in Edo State, Nigeria, I always had a strong feeling that God wanted me to be closer to Him. I knew that my Creator did not only desire a close relationship with me; He also wanted me to be involved in the kingdom business of soul-winning and in other services in His vineyard. God, through my mother, never left me in doubt about His plan for my life, and I indeed learned from my mother very early in life that God wanted me to be His emissary, propagating the Gospel of His dear Son, Jesus Christ. Nevertheless, I never gave God enough attention. I was far away from the Supreme Being, who was yearning for my companionship. I scorned God's invitation for a close association with Him because, then, I thought naively that walking with God would deny me opportunities to achieve those things I wanted to achieve in life and, above all, I would not be able to enjoy life. How wrong was I? Indeed, a counterforce of worldliness and acute hedonism took a strangulating hold on my life. I lived a pleasure-seeking lifestyle, which kept me away from God. The end result of my terrible lifestyle was that I kept rebuffing God's plans for my life and His request that I be in a relationship with Him and walk by His side.

However, today, I give glory to the Almighty God, who has rescued me from the forces of hedonism and sin, which for many years arrested my attention and diverted me away from God and His plan for my life. Today, I can celebrate the victory of Jesus Christ, on my behalf, over Satan and his evil forces that have for many years denied me the opportunity to have close association with God as a result of sin. Indeed, God never gave up on me. He was very persistent in His call to me, always seeking ways of rescuing me from the ruinous path on which I was treading in order for Him to achieve His purposes for my life.

Unfortunately, today, many people are in the same position as I was before I was rescued by His grace. Many people are daily turning down God's invitation for a life-long walk with Him. They are running away from a meaningful and destiny-changing relationship with their creator, following their own thoughts and their own ways. In the words of Prophet Isaiah, they are **"like sheep have gone astray; we have turned every one to his own way; and the Lord hath laid on him the iniquity of us all. Isaiah 53:6.**

The consequences of this straying away from God's chosen path for our lives are calamitous. The issue is that those whose God's heart is yearning for are still keeping the Almighty waiting for reciprocation of His agape love and response to His invitation to a life-long walk.

God Wants A Daily Walk With You

Dear Beloved Reader, I want you to know that God has always had the desire to have a relationship with you! Yes, the Almighty wants to associate with you even as you are reading this book. God is desirous of an everlasting, loving, and beneficial relationship with you and every other human being he has created. God had shown this holy desire of His at the beginning of all things when He created Adam in His image. God further revealed His love for the human race when "in the cool of the day", He usually comes down from heaven to the Garden of Eden in order to have a walk with Adam in the Garden.

And they heard the
voice of the Lord God
walking in the garden in
the cool of the day, and Adam
and his wife hid themselves from
the presence of the Lord God amongst
the trees in the garden. And the Lord God
called unto Adam and said unto him, Where
art thou? (Genesis 3:8–9 KJV)

Indeed, one of the reasons why God created you and me is that He wants to partner with us, associate with us, and be involved in our day-to-day lives. God wants to be our companion. The Almighty craves to engage in dialogue with you and me on several issues, especially those that relate to achieving our destinies. Your Creator is interested in walking with you so that He can be of help to you in the process of taking critical decisions that will determine the direction of your life and achieving your divine destiny.

From my personal experience, especially during those days when I excluded God from the decision-making process on issues that affected my life, I have realized that the consequences of walking in ways different from God's ways are disastrous. God wants to be involved in every matter of our lives; He wants to engage in dialogue with you; He wants intimacy with you; and He wants to be involved in your decision-making process. Little wonder then that He has been stretching forward His arms of love to you, inviting you to be His partner in the walk of life. Hence, I dare say that the ultimate desire of God is to have a daily walk with you on the journey of your life.

Will You Allow God To Walk With You?

God's desire to have a personal relationship with you comes from His amazing love and grace for you. Hear what Apostle John said about God's love for you:

> **"Behold, what manner of love the Father hath bestowed upon us, that we should be called the sons of God: therefore the world knoweth us not, because it knew him not. Beloved, now are we the sons of God, and it doth not yet appear what we shall be: but we know that, when he shall appear, we shall be like him; for we shall see him as he is. And every man that hath this hope in him purifieth himself, even as he is pure." (1 John 3:1–3 KJV).**

From this scripture, you can see that God's desire for a relationship with you is a function of His love for you. He knows that without you being connected to Him and without you engaging in a daily walk with Him, you cannot become what He wanted you to become in life when He created you. Believe it or not, you need God by your side as you daily grapple with the challenges of life and seek to achieve your life goals. It is rather sad that, just as many people are doing today, the first person, Adam, whom God sought to walk with, chose to spurn God's loving, caring, and wonderful offer of a lifelong relationship. He did this by disobeying God's commandment. His singular act of eating the forbidden fruit resulted in a sin that eventually separated mankind from God.

> **"Wherefore, as by one man sin
> entered into the world, and death by
> sin; and so death passed upon all men,
> for that all have sinned"
> (Romans 5:12)**

Yes, Adam's sin brought a breakdown in the relationship God has established with man, and the end result was regret, shame, and eternal punishment for humanity.

My beloved reader, as you are reading this book, God is offering you an invitation to a life-long walk with Him. Now is the time for you to respond to your Creator's invitation for a divine relationship that will shape and drive your life towards a successful end. If you decide to honor His invitation for a life-long walk, then you have done yourself a great favor. Indeed, you will be in good company with people like Enoch, Noah, Abraham, and many other Patriarchs of our faith who have walked with God during their lifetime. Among these patriarchs, Enoch was the first person to walk with God. All through the three hundred and sixty-five years. Enoch lived on earth; he walked with God in truth and righteousness. Indeed, the Bible declared that

> **"*Enoch walked with God;*
> and he was not, for God took
> him (Genesis 5:22–24 KJV).**

The aim of God's invitation for a life-long walk with you is to help you be successful in life here on earth and when you get to the Great Beyond. Hence, God does not only expect you to accept His invitation but to also walk with Him, as Enoch did. And you can rest assured that the Almighty God who empowered Enoch to walk with his Creator successfully is also ready to give you the ability and power to be successful as Enoch. What helped Enoch was his intense pursuit of holiness and righteousness, and this made him enjoy his walk with God. And God became so impressed with him that he took Enoch to heaven. If you too choose to walk with God, you will be taken to heaven, but that will be during the ultimate flight, the flight of the rapture of the saints, which you must not miss. During the flight, all those who have walked with God will have the Enoch experience and be transported to heaven in the power of the Holy Spirit to meet with our dear Lord Jesus Christ in the sky and welcome Him back.

The Essential Ingredients of A Daily Walk With God

1. Submit to the Lordship of Jesus Christ

A walk with God begins with the acceptance of Jesus Christ as one's personal Lord and Savior. The simple reason for this is that all human beings, including you and me, are fallen creatures consequent upon the sin of Adam and Eve in the Garden of Eden. And for us to associate with our holy Creator, we need to first and foremost be cleansed from our sins. Spiritual purgation is a prerequisite for a walk with God. It is the way in which we can be part of God's plan of redemption for humanity. This redemption comes through the shedding of the sinless blood of God's begotten Son, Jesus Christ. It is this holy blood of Jesus Christ that was shed on the Cross at Calvary that rescued us from our fallen state as condemned criminals who have been sentenced to a life jail in the place of eternal divine punishment created and reserved for sinners by God. That is the second death as a result of the sins of our first parents, Adam and Eve. Through Christ's supreme sacrifice, God elevated us and all those who will believe in Jesus Christ to the status of saints. We were rewarded with the right to everlasting life in heaven because of what Jesus Christ did. Once again, let's hear Apostle John speak on this matter:

Behold, what manner of love the Father has bestowed upon us, that we should be called the Sons of God: therefore the world knoweth us not, because it knew him not. Beloved, now are we the sons of God, and it does not yet appear what we shall be, but we know that, when he shall appear, we shall be like him, for we shall see him as he is. And every A man who has this hope in him purifies himself. even as he is pure. (1 John 3:1–3 KJV).

It is therefore the atoning death of Jesus Christ, the only begotten Son of God, that confers on us the qualification and the right to associate with and walk freely with God. Hence, the acceptance of the Lordship of Jesus Christ is a pre-requisite for walking with God. It is therefore imperative for you, dear reader, to accept Jesus Christ as your Lord and Savior today to enable you to enter into a glorious and life-long relationship and a walk with God.

Cry for a Rescue from the Power of Sin

For you to walk with God, you need to be rescued from sin. You need to admit that you are a sinner and confess your sins to God if you have not done so. Acknowledging your sinful state means being purely honest with God. It is about talking to him about the ways you lived your life without hiding anything or withholding anything from Him. And after confessing those sins, you must forsake them and do not go back to them.

Indeed, sin is very powerful. It is the potent weapon that Satan has been using and is still using today to enslave billions of people on earth and keep them on the Freeway to the place of eternal divine punishment created and reserved for sinners by God, where divine punishment awaits recalcitrant sinners. As a human being, you, dear reader, lack the capacity to free yourself from sin. No, you cannot rescue yourself from the spiritual power of sin. You need the help of a higher spiritual power to be free from this satanic power that has made disobeying God's laws and commands a routine and a daily habit for you. Apostle Paul, in his letter to early Christians in Rome, acknowledged this fact when he cried out for help in the Book of Romans. Let's hear him:

But I see another law among my members: warring. against the law of my mind, and bringing me into captivity to the law of sin, which is in my members. O wretched man that I am! Who shall deliver me from the body of this death? I thank God through Jesus. Christ is our Lord. So then, with my mind, I myself serve the law of God; but with the flesh, the law of sin. (Romans 7:23–24 KJV).

Here, Apostle Paul admitted his inability to do what is right, that is, to obey God, no matter how much he tried to do the will of God and obey His commandments. He always found himself in a state of enslavement to his sinful Adamic nature, with no hope of escape except when the Lord helped him. It follows, therefore, my dear reader, that you too need to cry out to God for help like Apostle Paul did so that you can be rescued from the power of sin.

Admitting your sins and forsaking them is very important. It is accepting your guilt as a sinner and deciding to turn to God, who is now saying, "This is the way to go; let's walk together in it." God is urging you today to come to him and engage him in discussions about the wrong things happening in your life and how to put them right. You therefore need to go to Him and own up to whatever you need to own up to. He is ever ready to shower His grace and love upon you, cleanse you from the dirt of sin, and empower you with newfound strength, resolve, and power to overcome sin.

Repent of all known sins.

At some point in life, as human beings, we are most likely to come to the realization that we are not what God wants us to be. We will realize that we are still far away from attaining our economic, social, and perhaps political goals. The realization of this fact and the desire to attain those goals that are yet to be achieved are the driving forces that propel us to work harder every day in order to attain our goals. This situation also applies to our spiritual lives. When we realize that our ways—the ways in which we live—do not please the Lord, at that stage it becomes imperative for us to have a rethink and a change of heart as well as amend our ways. This is where repentance comes in. In the Book of Second Corinthians, the Apostle Paul talked about admitting one's guilt and repentance:

> **Now I rejoice, not that you**
> **were made sorry, but that ye**
> **sorrowed to repentance: for ye**
> **were made sorry in a godly manner,**
> **that you might receive damage from us for nothing.**
> **For godly sorrow worketh repentance to salvation.**
> **not to be repented of, but the**
> **sorrow of the world works**
> **death. For behold this self-same**
> **thing, that ye sorrowed after a**
> **godly sort, what carefulness it wrought in you, yea,**
> **what clearing of yourselves, yea, what indignation,**
> **yea, what fear, yea, what vehement desire, yea,**
> **what zeal, yea, what revenge! In all things, you have**
> **approved yourselves to be clear in this matter.**
> **(2 Corinthians 7:9–11 KJV).**

Repentance is about change. It is taking full responsibility for your thoughts, actions, words, misdeeds, and all other things you have done, especially in not heeding the commandments of God. Repenting of your sins is about changing from your previous ways of thinking and living to new godly ways of life. Repentance involves recognizing and dealing with sin. Apostle John, in his letter, told us about the evil of sin. Let's hear John again."

> **And hereby, we do know that**
> **We know him if we keep his commandments.**

**He that saith, I know him, and keepeth
not his commandments,
is a liar, and the truth is not in him.
But whoso keeps his word?
In him verily is the love of God
perfected: hereby know we that we
are in him. He that saith he abideth in
him ought himself also to walk, even
as he walked. (1 John 2:3-6 KJV).**

Again, in chapter 5, John declared:

**"For this is the love of God,
that we keep his commandments:
and his commandments are not grievous."
(1 John 5:3 KJV).**

The driving force that propels you now will be your desire
to please God through your new way of life. Now, unlike
before, you want to live for God because you want to walk
with Him. In your new way of life, the godly way, all you
want is to commit yourself to reading the Bible, studying the
Word of God, and especially studying and understanding the
Gospel of our Lord Jesus Christ. Your desire now is to let God's
Word, the Bible, change your thinking and your life. Now
you will realize that walking in a way that lacks holiness and
is characterized by habitual sins will make God distant from
you. It removes you from the love, care, favor, mercy, and
protection of God. However, repentance and commitment to
the new godly way will secure your safety and open the lines
of communication and intimacy between you and God. Hence,
living a lifestyle of repentance is vital for you if you want to
walk daily with your Creator. When you begin to walk with

God, you will know that His ways are not like ours. You must yield to his lordship, guidance, and way of doing things. He must be allowed to call the shots, and you will only need to obey him and follow his instructions.

CHAPTER TWO

So Close to God, Yet Far Away From Him

During my days in the wilderness of sin, disobedience, and flagrant violation of God's commandments, my least concern was a relationship with my Creator. It wasn't that I hated God—no, far from it—but I just didn't care whether my acts of lasciviousness were pleasing to God or not. Yet right from the early years of my life, I have been a churchgoer because my mother ensured that I always accompanied her to church anytime she was going for a worship service or any other church program. As I grew up under my mummy's influence, I came to realize that she wanted me to have knowledge of God because she was a devoted Christian. Indeed, she was told that God had destined me right from the womb to be His servant. So, each time my mom called on me to get ready for church, I had no choice but to obey her and follow her to the church. So going to church was a routine thing for me, which I had to do in order to please my mother and be part of what was going on in the church.

However, as I grew older, I discovered that my interest in things of God diminished. Although I usually attend church services, I had very little interest in being closer to God. My attendance at church services was an opportunity for me to satisfy my ungodly lusts and cravings for women. My worship and services in the church were hollow. Unfortunately, many people are in this same position today. We have people in the church who attend church services regularly, pay their tithes, and give offerings, yet their hearts are far from God. They can speak in diverse tongues and even prophesy, but in their hearts, they are pretenders who do not belong to God. They are hypocrites. These people are deliberately holding back their hearts from God. No wonder the Lord called such people to order in the Book of Proverbs, chapter 23, when he declared thus:

> **My son, give me thine heart,**
> **and let thine eyes observe my**
> **ways. For a whore is a deep ditch;**
> **and a strange woman is a narrow pit.**
> **She also lieth in wait as for a prey,**
> **and increaseth the transgressors**
> **among men..**
> **(Proverb 23:26-28 KJV)**

Unfortunately, like I did before I met Christ, a lot of people in the church are holding back their hearts from God. They keep one foot in the church and the other foot in the world—in nightclubs and in bed with women of all shapes and sizes. Certainly, they cannot walk with God because they have no relationship with Him. They have no part in the kingdom of God. They can continue to go to church and participate in all the prayer meetings, worship services, and vigils, and be part of all church programs, yet they do not belong to Jesus Christ. Such people are so close to the eternal glory of God and yet so infinitely far from God's eternal joy and glory! In 2 Timothy Chapter 2, the Apostle Paul, in his letter to Timothy, declared:

> **Nevertheless the foundation of**
> **God standeth sure, having this seal, The**

Lord knoweth them that are his. And, Let every one that nameth the name of Christ depart from iniquity..." (2Timothy 2:19 KJV)

Those who are qualified to walk with God are those whose hearts, bodies, souls, and spirits have been surrendered to Jesus Christ. They are utterly sincere and faithful people who are not holding back their hearts and entire lives from their Creator. They are those who have gone to Calvary to surrender all to the Lord Jesus Christ at the cross. Yes, these are the people who are ready to give up their old ways of life so that they can begin to walk with God in the new way, which is Jesus Christ.

Dear reader, the question you should ask yourself is this: "Am I so close to God and yet so infinitely far from Him? This is a thought-provoking question that demands self-examination by every born-again Christian so that we can end our Christian journey the way Enoch ended his when he was transmuted into glory by God, who airlifted him into Paradise. It is sad today that we do have people in the church who are so close to God, yet they are far away from Him. These people are like their ilk in the Bible, such as Ananias and Sapphira, Gehazi, and even Judas Iscariot. These were people in Biblical times who, in spite of the fact that they had seen and tasted the power and glory of God, were far away from the Almighty God.

Let's go to the scriptures:

But a certain man named Ananias, with Sapphira his wife, sold a possession, And kept back part of the price, his wife also being privy to it, and brought a certain part, and laid it at the apostles' feet. But Peter said, Ananias, why hath Satan filled thine heart to lie

to the Holy Ghost, and to keep back part of the price of the land? Whilst it remained, was it not thine own? and after it was sold, was it not in thine own power? why hast thou conceived this thing in thine heart? thou hast not lied unto men, but unto God. And Ananias hearing these words fell down, and gave up the ghost: and great fear came on all them that heard these things. And the young men arose, wound him up, and carried him out, and buried him. And it was about the space of three hours after, when his wife, not knowing what was done, came in. And Peter answered unto her, Tell me whether ye sold the land for so much? And she said, Yea, for so much. Then Peter said unto her, How is it that ye have agreed together to tempt the Spirit of the Lord? behold, the feet of them which have buried thy husband are at the door, and shall carry thee out. Then fell she down straightway at his feet, and yielded up the ghost: and the young men came in, and found her dead, and, carrying her forth, buried her by her husband. And great fear came upon all the church, and upon as many as heard these things. (Acts 5:1-11 KJV)

Ananias and his wife, Sapphira, were members of the early church who accepted Jesus as their Lord and Savior, perhaps after listening to Apostle Peter's sermon on the Day of Pentecost, just like other Jewish believers. However, their hearts were far from God. They were neither truthful nor righteous. They wanted to walk with God half-heartedly, but the Holy Spirit would not allow that, and they paid the supreme price for it. There are many Ananias and Sapphiras in the church of God today. They want to hold back their old lifestyles from God instead of surrendering them all to Him. They want to have the advantage of the two worlds—one leg in the church and the other in the world. Yet God will have none of that. Another person is Gehazi, a son of the prophet, who was serving under the tutelage of a distinguished and heavily anointed prophet of God, Prophet Elisha. Gehazi could also be counted among the company of people like Ananias and Sapphira. Gehazi desired a walk with God through his association with Prophet Elisha, yet, in his heart, Gehazi harbored the spirit of greed and an inordinate desire for personal wealth.

And God could not tolerate Gehazi's filthy acts of greed, dishonesty, and unrighteousness. He and people of his character seemed to be close to God in their life-long walk with God, yet they were far away from Him. They cannot stay with God; He cannot tolerate them; rather, He will spit them out of His mouth, as the Lord said in the Book of Revelations:

**I know thy works, that thou
art neither cold nor hot: I would thou
wert cold or hot. So then because thou
art lukewarm, and neither cold nor hot, I will
spue thee out of my mouth (Revelations 3:15-16 KJV)**

The Lord, again, in the Book of Psalms, showed His aversion for those who want to walk with Him half-heartedly when He declared thus:

**For it was not an enemy
that reproached me; then I could
have borne it: neither was it he that hated
me that did magnify himself against me; then
I would have hid myself from him: But it was thou,**

a man mine equal, my guide, and mine acquaintance.
We took sweet counsel together, and walked
unto the house of God in company.
(Psalms 55:12-14—KJV)

God Wants A Relationship Built On Love And Obedience

Those whose hearts are far away from God do not have the spiritual capacity to walk with Him. They lack the character to be in the company of God. It is little wonder why they usually end up falling by the wayside. They could not walk with God because they were not ready to commit their bodies, souls, and spirits to the walk. Their walk with the Lord was not done wholeheartedly. There was a lack of diligent consecration on their part to the relationship God wanted to establish with them. God could not do any serious business with them because they lacked the qualities God was looking for in those who would be His partners in the lifelong walk. Yes, you may say that you do go to church or that you are even a pastor, a deacon, or a group leader in your church. But the question is: "Do you possess the wherewithal to be God's partner in the life-long walk?" Good enough, you are very active in your church, but are you truly and utterly sincere and faithful in your services to your Creator? These are the important issues to be considered. The kernel of our services to God is the relationship that exists between us and Him, and the basis of this relationship is the love He has for us. In the Book of John, the Bible declares:

God so loved the world that he gave his only begotten Son, that whosoever believeth in him should

LEARNING TO WALK WITH GOD LIKE ENOCH

**not perish, but have everlasting life. For God sent not
his Son into the world to condemn the world, but
that the world, through him, might be saved.
(John 3:16-17 KJV)**

Unlike what religion demands from us, God wants His
unconditional love for us reciprocated in the form of our love for
Him as well as our obedience to His rules and commandments.
He wants a personal rapport and a solid bond between us
and him. His desire for a close relationship with us is a result
of His love for us. This agape love is unqualified. It is not
contingent on our loyalty to Him or our actions. Indeed, it is
not a question of whether we deserve God's love or not. There
is no doubt that we do not really deserve God's love after we
have rebelled against Him in the Garden of Eden through our
progenitors—Adam and Eve.

Nevertheless, God loves us because it is in His nature to love.
When we begin to have a personal relationship with God, life
will start to be meaningful to us, and then we can really engage
Him in a life-long walk. We will then have a supreme and
reliable partner who will help us walk through the dark alleys
of life with our hands firmly held by Him. We will not need to
go through life blindly because "the light of the world" is with
us. In the book of John, the Scriptures declare thus:

**In him was life, and life was the light of men.
And the light shineth in darkness, and the darkness
comprehended it. (John 1:4-5 KJV)**

The Lord Jesus Christ Himself declared that He indeed is the
light of the world that illuminates the darkness of the world.
With Him by your side, as you continue the journey of life,

walking by His side, there is no groping in the dark because He will shed light on every darkness in your life. And every one whose life is rooted in Him need not entertain any worry or fear whatsoever.

**Then Jesus spoke again to them, saying, I am
the light of the world: he that followeth me shall
not walk in darkness, but shall have the light of life.
(John 8:12 KJV)**

To tell the truth, God knows us better than we or anyone else knows about us. He knows our beginning, our past, our present, and our future. He knows our needs, and only He knows how to meet them. He is the all-conquering warrior who fights our battles for us. He is the one who silences the roaring and devouring of evil lions in our foundations. He is the only one who can deal with the wicked powers of our fathers' and mothers' houses. We Africans know the level of havoc these wicked human and spiritual entities have done to the glorious destinies of millions of people on our continent and elsewhere in the world.

To prove that God yearns for a relationship with us and that He is always willing to help and save us, God, through His Son, the Lord Jesus Christ, sent out an invitation to all mankind, inviting us into a deep association with Him because only by associating with Him can we be delivered from demonic yokes and burdens that are militating against the achievement of our divine destinies. Listen to the Lord Jesus Christ's invitation:

**Come unto me, all ye that labour
and are heavy laden, and I will give you rest.
Take my yoke upon you, and learn of me; for I am**

meek and lowly in heart: and ye shall find rest unto your souls. For my yoke is easy, and my burden is light. (Mathew 11:28-30 KJV)

It goes without saying, therefore, that the best investment we can make in our lives is to develop a strong relationship with our Maker. When we succeed in doing this, then we will have the capacity to develop and sustain healthy and meaningful relationships with our fellow human beings.

CHAPTER THREE

PREPARING TO WALK WITH GOD

When the walk between God and Jacob got to a critical point, God demanded a review and strengthening of the relationship between Him and Jacob. The Almighty God deemed it fit to give the relationship a fresh impetus; therefore, He summoned a meeting between Him and Jacob and his household. The import of the important divine meeting was not lost on Jacob. He knew that this was not just an ordinary meeting but a very crucial one where the partnership between him and Jehovah God would be taken to a higher level. Hence, Jacob summoned a meeting before the meeting. The meeting before the divine meeting was between Jacob and members of his household. Now, let's go to the Bible:

> **And God said unto Jacob, Arise, go up to Bethel, and dwell there: and make there an altar unto God, that appeared unto thee when thou fleddest from the face of Esau thy brother. Then Jacob said unto his household, and to all that were with him, Put away the strange gods that are among you, and be clean, and change your garments: And let us arise, and go up to Bethel; and I will make there an altar unto God, who answered me in the day of my distress, and was with me in the way which I went. And they gave unto Jacob all the strange gods which were in their hand, and all their earrings which**

were in their ears; and Jacob hid them under the oak which was by Shechem. (Genesis 35:1-4 KJV)

The implication of Jacob's experience is that a walk with God is not a tea party. It is something that requires good preparation and planning. It is a lifetime walk that deserves the utmost care and caution. It is impossible to walk with God without meeting God's requirements. Among these requirements is putting away every foreign god that is in your life. **Foreign** gods are abominations to God. They provoke the Almighty God to jealousy and anger, as we see in Deuteronomy chapter 32:

> **But Jeshurun waxed fat and**
> **kicked: Thou art waxen fat, thou art**
> **grown thick, thou art covered with fatness;**
> **then he forsook God, who made him, and lightly**
> **esteemed the rock of his salvation.**
> **They provoked him**
> **to jealousy with strange gods, and**
> **abominations provoked**
> **him to anger. They sacrificed unto**
> **devils, not to God; to gods**
> **whom they knew not; to new**
> **gods that came newly up,**
> **whom your fathers feared not.**
> **(Deuteronomy 32:16–18 (KJV).**

No one can walk with God with contraband goods in his or her luggage. No, it is not possible that you cannot walk with God with all manner of sins—which are foreign gods—still in your life. You need to put them aside, as members of Jacob's household did before they left Shechem for Bethel. You must do away with every work of the flesh, which Apostle Paul listed in

EMMANUEL S. OMERE

Galatians Chapter 5, before you can begin and enjoy the life-long walk with God. Let's listen to Apostle Paul:

> Now the works of the
> flesh are manifest, which are
> these; Adultery, fornication, uncleanness,
> lasciviousness, Idolatry, witchcraft, hatred,
> variance, emulations, wrath, strife, seditions,
> heresies, Envyings, murders, drunkenness, revellings,
> and such like: of the which I tell
> you before, as I have also
> told you in time past, that they
> which do such things shall
> not inherit the kingdom of God.
> (Galatians 5:19–21 KJV).

If your preparations for your walk with God are not satisfactory to the Almighty, He will not sanction them. Even if he allows it, you cannot enjoy the journey.

Those who are ill-prepared for a walk with God cannot enjoy Jehovah God's blessings, mercy, favor, protection, and all kinds of goodness that come from him. Such people will pray, and their prayers will not be answered. They will seek God, but He will hide His face from them. Hear what the Lord told such people in the scriptures:

> And he said, I will hide my face
> from them; I will see what their end shall
> be, for they are a very froward generation,
> children in whom there is no faith. They have moved
> me to jealousy with that which is not God; they have
> provoked me to anger with their vanities; and

**I will move them to jealousy with those who
are not people; I will provoke them
to anger with a foolish nation.
(Deuteronomy 32:20–21 KJV)**

Again, in the Book of Isaiah, hear what the Lord told the impervious children of Israel:

**But your iniquities have
separated between you and your God,
and your sins have hid his face from you, that he
will not hear. For your hands are defiled with blood,
and your fingers with iniquity;
your lips have spoken lies,
your tongue hath muttered perverseness.
(Isaiah 59: 2-3 KJV).**

Dear reader, are you ready to walk with the Lord as Enoch did? Well, all you have to do to walk with your Creator and do it successfully is put aside all the foreign gods in your bags. You do not need to still hang on to those gods and idols because they will constitute roadblocks to you in the course of your journey with God. And mind you, anything can become a god that will hinder your walk with God. And talking about foreign gods, their identities are not hidden, as Apostle Paul revealed in his letter to the early Christians in Galatia. They are whatever gains your attention and devotion more than your creator. Whatever habit or work of the flesh that will hinder your relationship with the Almighty God is a foreign god that must be put aside and buried, as Joseph buried all the foreign gods he retrieved from the members of his family. These foreign gods may be pride of heart and arrogance, inordinate love of money, wealth, property, business, power, clothes, vehicles, fame, family, sex, alcohol, drugs, et cetera. Indeed, it is important, as a person who wants to walk with God, for you to live a life of holiness. You have to live a life that is consecrated to God because the One you want to walk with is a holy God.

Now, is there a god in your life that undermines your total and complete devotion to the Almighty God? If so, as members of Jacob's family, you must also surrender all those gods of sins to Jesus Christ so that He can bury them at Calvary. God is looking for people who are ready to separate themselves from the world and sin. Jehovah God is a holy God; hence, He can only walk with those who are perfect and spotless. These are the people who can be His partners in the journey of life. While we accept the fact that you cannot make yourself spotless and wrinkle-free, you can access the precious blood of Jesus Christ that was shed at Calvary. He is always ready to purify and sanctify you.

How to Prepare to Walk with God.

1. Get God Involved in Every Decision and Choice You Make, No Matter How Insignificant

God is interested in everything we do, our thoughts and actions, as well as the choices and decisions we make on all matters affecting our lives, at all times, no matter how little they may seem to us. As far as God is concerned, nothing about our lives is inconsequential. Everything about us matters to Him. Fundamentally, this attitude of God is a consequence of His love and care for us. The depth of God's love for us is unfathomable, and He cares so much for us, even about the little details we may want to ignore. God is interested in every little thing about our lives, such that He even numbered the hairs on our heads! The Lord Jesus Christ confirmed this in His teaching in the Book of Luke:

> **Are not five sparrows sold for two farthings, and not one of them is forgotten before God? But even the very hairs of your head are all numbered. Fear not therefore: ye are of more value than many sparrows. (Luke 12:6-7 KJV)**

We can now see that God wants us to depend on Him at all times. He wants us to depend on Him for all our needs in all situations. As a matter of fact, He wants us to get our daily bread from Him. And He has assured us that He will never leave us or forsake us, all along the way.

> **Let your conversation be without covetousness; and be content with such things as ye have: for he hath said, I will never leave thee, nor forsake thee. So that we may boldly say, The Lord is my helper, and I will not fear what man shall do unto me.. (Hebrews 13:5–6 KJV)**

We need to involve God closely in everything we do on a daily basis. Every aspect of our lives must be driven by our love and deep affection for God and a burning desire to be close to Him and obey Him.

2. You Must Learn To Appreciate Everything. God Has Done For Us

There is no human being that detests being praised for any good deed he or she did. Commendations for great exploits are seen as motivation that will spur people to do more good. A good example here is the relationship between husband and wife. Words of encouragement and commendations are instruments for deepening the conjugal bond between couples. The same is true of the relationship between us and our heavenly Father. Jehovah God also wants us to always show our appreciation to Him for all His innumerable goodness to us. And by expressing our joy, happiness, and gratitude to Him, we can strengthen the bond between us and our Father in heaven. In the Book of First Thessalonians, Apostle Paul counseled us thus:

In everything, give thanks, for this is the will of God in Christ Jesus, concerning you (I Thessalonians 5:18 KJV)

Our daily experiences and the various challenges of life that come our way from time to time provide several opportunities for us to demonstrate our deep love, affection, and appreciation to God for His goodness in our lives. As we surmount the storms of life, such as afflictions, sicknesses, and other fiery arrows aimed at us by Satan, our arch enemy, it is indeed imperative for us to express gratitude to our Defender and unmovable Pillar and Shelter in the storms of life.

With songs of praise and worship, we should let God, our anchor, know that we are thankful to Him for all He is doing for us. We must not fail to regularly express our heartfelt gratitude to our heavenly Father, Jehovah God, His Son, the Lord Jesus Christ, as well as to the wonderful counselor and our bulwark of defense, the Holy Spirit. When we make it a habit to praise the Lord and express our appreciation to Him every day, we will be strengthening the bond between us and

God. It is then that we can talk about having a solid relationship with our Creator.

3. Express Your Faithfulness Through Your Actions

The proof of our faith and trust in God is usually demonstrated in the choices and decisions we make at critical times in our lives. When the billowing storms of life assail our peace and comfort, do we still remain on the side of Jesus Christ? Do we not look for the easy way out of difficult situations even when we know that God will never approve the choices we are making? Indeed, we can be closely connected with God through the practical demonstration of our faithfulness, loyalty, and obedience to Him when we are faced with the vicissitudes of life. That is the time to demonstrate our unconditional love for God. The degree of our faithfulness and loyalty to God is demonstrated when we find ourselves in dire straits. As children of God who desire a strong relationship with Him, we must prove to Him that we are His and will always be on His side, irrespective of the circumstances in which we find ourselves.

Just as Daniel did by daring Babylon's devouring lions and electing to pray to His God instead of King Darius's royal statue (Daniel 6:10–11), we must let the love we have for God manifest in the choices we make when we are in difficult situations. We must know that when we choose to endure sufferings and deprivations in order not to offend God but rather make Him happy, even as the three Hebrew youths—Meshach, Shedrack, and Abednego—did, then we are telling our God that we are His and we can be trusted just as he trusted Job. We can then boldly declare, as Apostle Paul said in the Book of Romans, that nothing and absolutely nothing can separate us from Him.

**What shall we then say to these
things? If God be for us, who can be against
us? He that spared not his own Son, but delivered
him up for us all, how shall he
not with him also freely
give us all things? Who shall lay
any thing to the charge
of God's elect? It is God that justifieth.
Who is he that condemneth?
It is Christ that died, yea rather, that is risen
again, who is even at the right hand of God,
who also maketh intercession for us. Who
shall separate us from the love of Christ? shall
tribulation, or distress, or persecution, or
famine, or nakedness, or peril, or sword?
(Romans 8:31–35 KJV)**

When we live our lives in a way that shows that we have high spiritual integrity, then God will surely consider us to be His own, and He can vouch for us as He did for Job (Job 1:8). He can then proudly call us his sons and daughters. In our time of need, we too can confidently rely on God for help, even as we have the right to rely on and claim His promises to us in the scriptures.

4. You Must Rely On His Infinite Power. To Meet Your Needs

In the Book of Matthew, the Lord Jesus admonishes us thus:

**Therefore, I say unto you, Take no thought for your life.
what ye shall eat, or what ye shall drink; nor yet for your
body, what ye shall put on. Is not life more than meat?**

and the body than theraiment? Behold the fowls of the air, for
They sow not, neither do they reap, nor gather into barns.
yet your heavenly Father feeds them. Are you not much better than they? Which of you, by taking thought, can add one cubit to his stature? And why take your thought for raiment? Consider the lilies of the field and how they grow; they
toil not, nor do they spin. And yet I say unto you,
Even Solomon, in all his glory, was not arrayed like one. of these. Therefore, if God so clothes the grass of the field, whichto day is, and to morrow is cast into the oven, shall he not much more clothe you, O ye of little faith? Therefore take no thought, saying, What shall we eat? or, What shall we drink? or, Wherewithal shall we be clothed? (For after All these things do the Gentiles seek: for your heavenly Father knows that you have a need for all these things. But seek
ye first the kingdom of God, and his righteousness; and All these things shall be added to you. Take therefore No thought for the morrow; for the morrow shall take thought for the things themselves. Sufficient for the day is the evil thereof. (Mathew 6:25-33 KJV).

Here Jesus counsels believers in Him to cast their burdens upon Him and stop worrying themselves about the needs and pressures of life. Indeed, we Christians can save ourselves from unnecessary agonies and anxieties by relying on the Almighty God, who provides for and takes perfect care of inconsequential animals like birds as well as plants. If we do, He will surely provide for our needs at the right time. But many people are too busy in a hurry. They cannot wait for God's time, whereas

God does His own things at His own time; God's time is the right time. The Bible declares in Ecclesiastes that God's time is the perfect time, and that is the time we must wait for—the time He perfects all things for His beloved. Hear the preacher:

**He hath made every thing beautiful
in his time: also he hath set the world in their
heart, so that no man can find out the work that God
maketh from the beginning to the
end. (Ecclesiastes 3:11 KJV)**

Indeed, it is important for us to put our trust in God and allow him to direct every step we take. When difficult situations come, we can rest assured that we will not be alone. In the book of Proverbs, the Bible again tells us to put our trust in Him:

**Trust in the Lord with all thine heart;
and lean not unto your own understanding.
In all your ways, acknowledge him,
and he shall direct your paths.
(Proverbs 3:5–6 KJV)**

In the Book of Psalm, the Psalmist also harped on the need to put our confidence in Him, who is the God of all flesh and for whom nothing is impossible:

**"Trust in the Lord, and do good; so shalt thou dwell.
in the land, and verily thou shalt be fed. Delight thyself
also in the Lord, and he shall give you the desires of your
heart. Commit thy way unto the Lord; trust also in
him; and
He shall bring it to pass (Psalm 37:3-5 KJV).**

5. Study And Meditate On The Word Of God Daily

**"If we live in the Spirit, let us also walk in the Spirit."
(Galatians 5:25 KJV)**

Believers' relationship with God is based on their knowledge
of who God is and their daily interactions with Him as friends.
It's a two-way love affair. For us to deepen this relationship,
we need daily interaction with God, and where this interaction
can take place is in the Bible. Hence, believers who have little
interest in reading and studying the Bible cannot enjoy God.
It is in the Bible that God tells us all we need to know about
Him. It is in His Word that we can find the secrets of a life-
long successful walk with the Lord, just like Enoch did. God's
divine rendezvous takes place in the Bible. So we must make
the Bible the place to visit and interact with God and where He
can speak to us. and we in turn speak to Him on a daily basis.

6. You must always create.
Time to Pray

God is always available for us, and He is willing and eager to
talk to us. There is no doubting the fact that we can't build a
strong relationship with God if we don't converse with Him
daily and as often as possible. Two friends who communicate
with each other sparingly cannot be considered good friends.
And God wants us to be good friends. The same is true for
couples too, because husbands and wives who do not maintain
regular communication at home will always have strained
relationships. We can now imagine the consequences of our
failure to talk to God through prayers on a regular basis. God
should be number one in our lives, and we should not allow
anything to come between us and God in terms of prayers. In

the Book of Jeremiah, God made it known to us His children that He always likes to talk to us; He cherishes conversation between us and Him.

Call unto me, and I will answer you, and she will thee great and mighty things, which thou knowest not (Jeremiah 33:3 KJV)

In the Book of Isaiah, the Lord assured us that our conversation with Him would never be a talk to the air or a monologue.

And it shall come to pass that before they call, I will answer, and while they are yet speaking, I will hear (Isaiah 65:24 KJV).

My dear reader, you can begin to converse with God today. It's never too late. Begin to talk to your Maker today in prayer and join billions of people who have been enjoying wonderful experiences in prayer to the Almighty God. Know surely that as you give quality time to God in prayer and in reading and studying His Word, He will surely get closer and closer to you.

CHAPTER FOUR

BENEFITS AND JOY IN A
PERSONAL WALK WITH GOD

A part from the salvation of my soul, the value of which cannot be measured in terms of trillions of dollars, the Lord Jesus Christ has done so much for me as a result of my daily walk with Him. I have reaped so many benefits from my association with the Lord Jesus, many of which I cannot remember. His goodness to me is immeasurable. How can I thank Him enough for annulling medical doctors' verdict of death for me when I was given just three months to live and died after being afflicted by a chronic cancer by powers of darkness? (The full story of my cancer ailment and my miraculous healing is in another book produced by Omere Evangelical & Soul-Wining Ministries.) God healed me, and I became perfectly free of cancer, to the astonishment of cancer experts at the Boston Medical Cancer Centre, who had expected me to die of chronic cancer. What more can I ask for? Indeed, I owe him an eternal debt of gratitude, praise, worship, and consecration to His service. This wonderful and glorious God, who has been my partner in the journey of life and has done and is still doing great things for me and my family, On several occasions, I had come face-to-face with death, both physically and in my dreams. He has fought so many spiritual battles for me and vanquished Satan, the enemy of my soul, on my behalf. I escaped death by being crushed by a fast-moving trailer on a highway while I was crossing the road. The Lord, in His mercy, rescued me. Indeed, I cannot recount all that my merciful, kind, and caring God has done for me and my family. There are so many.

However, there is one experience that stands out among the several I have had in the course of my walk with God. Some time ago, one of my children got into trouble with the police over a matter she knew nothing about. Every fact of the case, when critically examined, established the innocence of my daughter. Indeed, I was convinced in my heart that my daughter knew nothing about the offense she was alleged to have committed. Nevertheless, the police would not accept our argument of innocence, so they opted to charge her in court, and before we knew it, we had a serious matter in our hands.

In spite of the decision of the police to charge her in court, I was never perturbed because, by then, I had given my life to Jesus Christ and had already started walking with Him as well as serving in His vineyard as a minister of the gospel. So even though I knew quite alright that my daughter was at risk of going to jail, I had solid faith in the Almighty God whom I was serving, and I believed that He would prove my daughter's innocence and deliver her from evil. In Psalm 46, God gave solid assurances of defense, protection, and care for all those who are walking with Him with an upright heart. Let's go to the Bible:

God is our refuge and strength, a very present help in trouble. Therefore, we will not fear, though the earth be removed, and though the mountains be carried into the midst of the sea, though the waters thereof roar and be troubled, though the mountains shake with the swelling thereof. Selah.
(Psalm 46:1–3 KJV)

God Is A Place Of Refuge For You.

God was a solid place of refuge for me and my family in our time of need. There was nowhere else to go and no one else to turn to except my Creator. And when I took my daughter's case to Him, after several sessions of intense prayers and supplications, He answered me. The Lord used my senior pastor for me, as he gave me moral and spiritual support. The two of us went to the Christian Prayer Center in New Hampshire, where we spent days in fervent prayers interceding for my daughter. In the Book of Nahum, the Lord, through Prophet Nahum, declared thus:

**The Lord is good, a strong hold
in the day of trouble; and he knoweth
them that trust in him. But with an overrunning
flood he will make an utter end of the place thereof,
and darkness shall pursue his enemies.
(Nahum 1:7-8KJV).**

Almighty God proved Himself to be my impregnable refuge in my days of trouble. He was my stronghold that the enemy, Satan, could not overrun. Hallelujah! The Lord fought for me, and my daughter was eventually discharged and acquitted after the court established her innocence. What more can I say about this God who is ever faithful to those who are ready to walk with him in purity and holiness?

My dear reader, all these things that God did for me are incomparable with the great benefits that will accrue to you if you decide to engage your Creator in a life-long walk. He is eagerly waiting to be your partner and walk along with you, with your hand firmly held in His own big hands as He walks you through the rough paths of life, unscathed by the vicissitudes of life.

He Is Never Far Away From Us.

The moment a person accepts the message of salvation in the Gospel of our Lord Jesus Christ, such a person is born anew into the family of God. The next thing that follows is to develop a relationship with God so that the new convert can grow spiritually daily in the course of walking with Him and consequently enjoy the full benefits of becoming a redeemed disciple of the Lord, who is always walking by His side. This relationship, which is fostered by the Holy Spirit, is very, very crucial for every child of God who has been genuinely redeemed by the precious blood of the Lamb of God—Jesus Christ—and who desires a life-long walk with God.

Owing to the fact that we believers cannot do without the closeness and support of the Lord Jesus, in our daily walk with and growth in the Lord, the Lord Jesus, our Savior, Friend, Redeemer, and Father, assured us at the time of His departure that because He loves us dearly, He will always be with us and that we will never be abandoned like orphans:

"I will not leave you comfortless:
I will come to you. Yet a little while,
and the world seeth me no more; but
ye see me: because I live, ye shall live
also (John 14:18-19 KJVK)

Even though He was physically departing the planet earth, the Lord Jesus assured us that He would never be far away from us, because the relationship that started on the cross, where He died and did the work of our redemption, as well as our own confession and acceptance of Him as our Redeemer, Lord, and Saviour, must continue and be sustained. Hence the promise of the Holy Spirit, the Comforter and Helper Who will help us to walk successfully with God in the journey of life:

> **These things have I spoken unto**
> **you, being yet present with you. But**
> **the Comforter, which is the Holy Ghost,**
> **whom the Father will send in my name, he**
> **shall teach you all things, and bring all things**
> **to your remembrance, whatsoever I have said**
> **unto you. (John 14:25–26 KJV).**

Again in Chapter 16 of the Book of John, the Lord Jesus further stressed the importance of the role of the Holy Spirit in helping us to build and sustain a strong relationship with God so that we can walk successfully with Him:

> **Nevertheless I tell you the truth;**
> **It is expedient for you that I go away:**
> **for if I go not away, the Comforter will**
> **not come unto you; but if I depart, I will**
> **send him unto you. And when he is come,**
> **he will reprove the world of sin, and of**
> **righteousness, and of judgment: Of sin,**
> **because they believe not on me;**
> **(John 16:7-9 KJV)**

Holy Spirit, an Indispensable
Helper The Journey of Life

When the Holy Spirit, the counselor, takes residence in the
body and life of a believer, then the major ingredient needed in
building a personal relationship with God has been acquired.
And from that moment on, the process of building and
strengthening personal relationships with God began. Such
a person has the confidence to look forward to a successful
walk with His Creator. Every day, the Holy Spirit will order
our steps in our daily walk with God. He will counsel us,
teach us, and direct our thoughts, utterances, and actions as
the relationship between us and God continues to grow. Little
wonder, Apostle Paul declared thus in his letter to Christians
in Rome:

**For as many as are led by
the Spirit of God, they are the sons
of God. For ye have not received the spirit
of bondage again to fear; but ye have received
the Spirit of adoption, whereby we cry, Abba, Father.
The Spirit itself beareth witness
with our spirit, that we
are the children of God: And if
children, then heirs; heirs
of God, and joint-heirs with Christ;
if so be that we suffer
with him, that we may be also glorified together.
(Romans 8:14-17 KJV)**

As we continue to grow in the Lord, day by day, walking with
Him with the help of the Holy Spirit, God, through His Spirit

that lives in us, will continue to work on us so that our lives can be transformed into what He wants us to be in order to conform to the image of His dear Son, Jesus Christ. Without the Holy Spirit, we would not have the ability to grow in the Lord, and we could not enjoy the huge benefits of walking with God. It is the Holy Spirit who will help us shun evil and temptations whenever they come our way. It is the Holy Spirit that will help us undergo the much-needed spiritual transformation. As we grow in the Lord, get to know Him more and more, and become closer to Him in our daily walk with Him, His Spirit in us will help us to produce the fruits that befit us as the children of the Most High. Our daily conduct in all ways will begin to manifest the characters and behaviors of genuinely born-again Christians. These are the fruits of the Holy Spirit that Apostle Paul enumerated in his letter to early Christians in the Book of Galatia:

**But the fruit of the Spirit is love,
joy, peace, longsuffering, gentleness,
goodness, faith, Meekness, temperance:
against such there is no law. And they that
are Christ's have crucified the flesh with the
affections and lusts. If we live in the Spirit, let
us also walk in the Spirit. (Galatians 5:22–25 KJV).**

God has always desired the restoration of the wonderful union He had with mankind in the Garden of Eden before Adam and Eve fell into sin of disobedience. Through His amazing love and kindness, God engineered this process of reconciliation of humanity to Himself through the sacrificial death of His Son, Jesus Christ. He thus re-established the lost personal relationship that He had with humanity, which Adam and Eve enjoyed with Him in Eden. Today, God is asking for a similar relationship with every believer in the Lord Jesus Christ.

Hence, any believer who does not have a personal relationship with God does not know Him; he or she cannot walk with God. He or she cannot enjoy the fruits of walking with God because such a person is not a child of God. Jesus Christ died so that we could have a living and functional relationship with God. The intimacy and companionship God desires from us is not the one engendered by the foreboding fear of running afoul of God's laws or a relationship that we are compelled into because we have an obligation to keep God's commandments. Absolutely, that is not the kind of relationship God wants.

The relationship I am talking about here is the one that is built purely on the love we have for God. That is the only relationship that can make walking with God beneficial to us and make our lives meaningful. There is no doubting the fact that God loves us. Amazingly, in spite of our frailties, God's agape love for us never wanes. God can never stop loving us. Therefore, the least we can do to appreciate His love, mercy, favor, and kindness is to love Him in return. The basis of this love is that we belong to the Commonwealth of Redeemed People, whose salvation was purchased by the precious blood of the Lamb of God, Jesus Christ. Apostle John confirmed God's love for us in Scripture:

> **"Behold, what manner of love**
> **the Father hath bestowed upon us,**
> **that we should be called the sons of God:**
> **therefore the world knoweth us not, because**
> **it knew him not. Beloved, now are we the sons**
> **of God, and it doth not yet appear what we shall**

be: but we know that, when he shall appear, we shall be like him; for we shall see him as he is. And every man that hath this hope in him purifieth himself, even as he is pure." (1 John 3:1–3 KJV).

The essence of our salvation is to get reconnected to God, to be reconciled with Him, to begin to relate to Him intimately, and for Him to be the pivot around which our lives revolve. Christianity is about developing a personal relationship with God. The Almighty God wants us to love Him and be in a deep relationship with Him.

Walking in Love With God

Our relationship with God should be founded on love for Him and not on the fact that we need Him for sustenance. Every man and woman created by God needs to cultivate a relationship with his or her creator out of love for Him. God Himself has initiated the process of this wonderful relationship with Him by sacrificing His Son, Jesus Christ, who removed and destroyed every hindrance that can bock our way to God. Now, God wants a perfect father-son or father-daughter relationship with us. It is the burning desire of God that humanity should live in oneness and love with Him.

Behold, I will gather them out of all countries, whither I have driven them in my anger, in my fury, and in great wrath, and I will bring them again to this place, and I will cause them to dwell safely. And they shall be my people, and I will be their God. And I will Give them one heart and one way that they may fear. forever, for the good of them and of their children.

after them (Jeremiah 32:37–39 KJV).

In John 3:16, God demonstrated to us the love that He wants to share with us, always in an intimate relationship with him. It is this perfect love that made God sacrifice His only Son for us:

> **"For God so loved the world, that
> he gave his only begotten Son, that
> whosoever believeth in him should not
> perish, but have everlasting life. For God
> sent not his Son into the world to condemn
> the world; but that the world through him might
> be saved. (John 3:16 KJV).**

We must therefore not base our relationship with God on anything else other than pure love for Him. The Lord Jesus loves us, and His love is unconditional. It is not based on our faithfulness or the level of our spiritual devotion to Him. Rather, Jesus just loves us and wants to be close to us. He desires an intimate relationship with us in spiritual union with Him. In the Book of John, the Lord Jesus gave us a picture of the kind of relationship He wants to have with us:

> **"I am the true vine, and my Father is the
> husbandman. Every branch in me that beareth not
> fruit he taketh away: and every branch that beareth
> fruit, he purgeth it, that it may bring forth more
> fruit. Now ye are clean through the word which I
> have spoken unto you. Abide in me, and I in you.
> As the branch cannot bear fruit of itself, except it
> abide in the vine; no more can ye, except ye abide
> in me. I am the vine, ye are the branches: He that
> abideth in me, and I in him, the same bringeth forth**

much fruit: for without me ye can do nothing. If a
man abide not in me, he is cast forth as a branch,
and is withered; and men gather them, and cast
them into the fire, and they are burned. If ye abide
in me, and my words abide in you, ye shall ask what
ye will, and it shall be done unto you. Herein is my
Father glorified, that ye bear much fruit; so shall
ye be my disciples. As the Father hath loved me,
so have I loved you: continue ye in my love. If ye
keep my commandments, ye shall abide in my love;
even as I have kept my Father's commandments,
and abide in his love. These things have I spoken
unto you, that my joy might remain in you, and
that your joy might be full. (John 15:1-11 KJV).

The kernel of our personal relationship with God is the union
between us and His Son, Jesus Christ. In His letter to early
Christians in the City of Corinth, Apostle Paul spoke about
the uniqueness of the relationship that exists between the Lord
Jesus Christ and the saints of God:

Know ye not that your bodies are
the members of Christ? shall I then take
the members of Christ, and make them
the members of an harlot?
God forbid. (1 Corinthians 6:15 KJV)

Also concerning the relationship between Jesus Christ and us
believers, Apostle Peter declared:

To whom coming, as unto a
living stone, disallowed indeed
of men, but chosen of God, and precious,

Ye also, as lively stones, are built up a spiritual house, an holy priesthood, to offer up spiritual sacrifices, acceptable to God by Jesus Christ. Christ (1 Peter 2:4-5 KJV).

It is therefore pertinent to note that if we are to fulfill the purposes for which God sent us into this world and, at the end of our tour of duty on planet Earth, have a place of rest in heaven where God lives, we must cultivate a strong personal relationship with God and walk with Him every day of our lives in truth and holiness. Without walking with God, we cannot fulfill the purposes for which we are here on planet Earth. We need God as our indispensable companion in the journey of life if we are to live a meaningful life. Putting our trust in God on a daily basis and relying on Him for our sustenance each day of our lives will help us to build and sustain personal relationships with Him. In addition, for us to establish, sustain, and nurture our relationship with our Maker, we need to live a prayerful life as well as become avid readers of the Bible so that we can know God intimately through the knowledge of His Word as well as with the help of the Holy Spirit.

CHAPTER FIVE

THE SECRET TO LIVING FOR AND WALKING WITH GOD

"I have fought a good fight,
I have finished my course, I have
kept the faith: Henceforth there is laid
up for me a crown of righteousness, which
the Lord, the righteous judge, shall give me
at that day: and not to me only, but unto all
them also that love his appearing."
(2 Tim. 4:7-8 KJV).

In the above scripture, Apostle Paul told us the story of how he overcame the challenges of life and all the darts of the enemy targeted at him to discourage him from his walk with God. Through his resilience, holy determination, and firmness of purpose, Apostle Paul triumphed over all the challenges that came his way and, at the end, he was able to prevail. As Apostle Paul discovered in his walk with God, one of the secret weapons we need to arm ourselves with in order to succeed in our walk with God is the grit determination to be holy. In the face of daunting challenges that can make us fall by the wayside in our walk with our creator, we need to be resilient in our determination to obey God's commandments and laws by living a life of holiness and righteousness.

In his second letter to the early Christians in the city of Corinth, the Apostle Paul stressed the importance of holiness and righteousness as potent weapons of defense in repulsing attacks from Satan and his evil forces, which are aimed at luring us into sins, and also in launching holy and lethal attacks against satanic powers even as we continue to work out our salvation every day **(see Philippians 2:12-14 KJV)** and relying on Jesus Christ to help us live a holy life. Hear the Apostle Paul speak on the armor of righteousness:

In stripes, in imprisonments, in tumults, in labours, in watchings, in fastings; By pureness, by knowledge, by longsuffering, by kindness, by the Holy Ghost, by love unfeigned, By the word of truth, by the power of God, by the armour of righteousness on the right hand and on the left, By honour and dishonour, by evil report and good report: as deceivers, and yet true; As unknown, and yet well known; as dying, and, behold, we live; as chastened, and not killed; As sorrowful, yet alway rejoicing; as poor, yet making many rich; as having nothing, and yet possessing all things. (2 Cor 6:5–10 KJV)

Indeed, there is no denying the fact that we need and must possess top-notch spiritual resilience and holy determination to be holy and righteous, as the Apostle Paul did, in order to overcome temptations and all kinds of assaults orchestrated against us by Satan and his evil forces. The aims of these attacks include, among others, their quest to dampen our desire to walk with God in holiness and righteousness. Satan hates holiness and righteousness, and he doesn't want Christians to possess these two virtues so that they can be susceptible to his attacks.

This reminds me of a subtle attack launched against my spiritual life by Satan some years ago. The major objective of the attack was to derail my walk with God and my newfound joy and peace in God. Satan attacked me in the area where he knew I was weak—women. However, unknown to him, my redeemer had already removed that weakness from my life. He had already strengthened me with his grace and power to overcome sexual sins and engage in immoral relationships.

There was a lady that I dated while I wasn't a born-again Christian. I dated the lady for five years before I quit the relationship. Something happened that made me have a severe relationship with her. In fact, I deleted her numbers from my phone. And what is more, when I was born again, I completely steered clear of her. I didn't talk to her again or have anything to do with her. But one day I went to the supermarket for shopping, and I ran into her. She was surprised to see me too, and she was obviously excited to see me.

"Why have you stayed away from me", she asked with a tinge of excitement in her voice. "Oh, I just decided to go for Christ. If you are not in Christ, then you are in crisis,", I exclaimed. I told her further that the life I was living before I met Christ was not good, and that wasn't the type of life God wanted me to live, so I had to change. I asked her too if she had met Christ, and she answered in the affirmative. She said she has joined **the Latter-Day Saints Church**, the church of Mormons. She appeared to want us to revive our relationship because she said she had missed the fun we used to have together when we were still dating each other. Before I cut off the relationship, almost every weekend, we used to visit one restaurant or another. It was a new restaurant per weekend. People even thought we were husband and wife.

So, she quickly wrote her mother's phone number on a piece of paper and asked me to call her as she was entering her car. And we parted ways. As I was walking back to my car, the Holy Spirit told me that I was on my way back to the world again. It then dawned on me that there was no way this lady would come to my house and that something would not happen between us. I then brought out the piece of paper containing her phone number, tore it into pieces, and put it in the trash. I then went back home.

Indeed, every decision we make to stand with God and walk with Him in holiness and righteousness will be subjected to a serious test by Satan and his evil forces. Nevertheless, we can overcome such tests by standing for holiness and righteousness, irrespective of the circumstances in which we find ourselves, by renewing our minds through reading and studying the Word of God, and by spending time with Jesus in prayer and meditation. This is what can help us build ourselves up, remain strong in our walk with God, and succeed in our lifelong walk with our Creator.

My dear, beloved reader, it behooves us as partners with God in the life-long walk with the Almighty to be watchful and always stand firm for holiness and righteousness. In everything we do, we need to be guided and directed by Biblical standards. We must resolutely pursue holiness and righteousness, no matter the circumstances in which we find ourselves, in order to make God happy. However, we must not be unaware of the fact that it is only God who can help us. With His help, our desire to attain holiness and righteousness will be met. Again, let us listen to the Apostle Paul speak:

**Not as though I had already attained it, either were
already perfect, but I follow after, if that I may apprehend.
that for which I am also apprehended by Christ Jesus.
Brethren, I count not myself to have apprehended:
but this one thing I do, forgetting those things which
are behind, and reaching forth unto those things which
are before, I press toward the mark for the prize of the
high calling of God in Christ Jesus.**

(Philippians 3:12–14 KJV)

It, therefore, goes without saying that as children of God, as
people who have been redeemed by the precious blood of the
Lamb of the righteous God and who are heaven-bound, the
issue of righteousness must be of great importance to us. It is
imperative for us to live a righteous life, a life that conforms to
God's standards of holiness, honesty, legality, and justice.

The Natural Man's Deficiency in
Living a Righteous and Holy Life

Owing to our depraved and sinful nature, which we inherited
from Adam and Eve, no human being has the innate capacity
to be righteous and holy. God, through the Apostle Paul, made
this known to us:

**As it is written, There is none righteous, no, not
one: There is none that understandeth, there is
none that seeketh after God. They are all gone.
out of the way, they have together become unprofitable;
there is none that doeth good, no, not one.
Romans 3:10–12 (KJV)**

Here, we have a problem. How do sinful people relate to the holy God? Indeed, without righteousness, we cannot truly serve God. By His very nature, God is righteous; hence, God cannot tolerate any form of unrighteousness from us. And this is the reason why, even while we were yet to key into God's plan of redemption for mankind and salvation from sin, God made a plan to rescue us from our guilt of unrighteousness and the commensurate punishment, which is eternal spiritual death and separation from God. Hear what the Bible says:

But God commends his love toward us in that. While we were yet sinners, Christ died for us. Much More then, being now justified by his blood, we shall be saved from wrath through him. If and when we were enemies, we were reconciled to God by the death of his Son, much more, being reconciled, we shall be saved by his life. Romans 5:8–10 (NKJV)

God, in His mercy, upon our acceptance of the finished work of redemption on the cross by Jesus Christ, declared us righteous. Thus, every sinner who confesses his or her sin and believes in Jesus Christ is declared righteous, that is, justified, by God the Father through Jesus Christ the Son, who died and paid for mankind's sins on the cross. Yes, we are made righteous; we became just people by virtue of the activities of the Holy Spirit, who is working daily in us to make us conform to God's standards of holiness and righteousness. Any unregenerated person, the natural man, who is still carnal in his thoughts, utterances, and deeds, cannot be righteous. The carnal man does not have the perfect righteousness of God. Let us hear what the prophet Isaiah says:

But we are all unclean things, and all
Our righteousness is as filthy rags, and
We all do fade as a leaf, and our iniquities,
like the wind, have taken us away.
Isaiah 64:6 King James Version (KJV)

A Call to Righteousness

Righteousness is about living your life for God. It is about dedicating your life to living a righteous life; it is about doing the will of God in all ways at all times. Righteousness is about living your life to please God here on earth so that you can inherit the kingdom of God. Indeed, everyone who accepts Jesus Christ as his or her personal savior is born into God's family with the hope of eternal life. And as a redeemed son of the Lord who is genuinely saved, you belong to that family. And to retain your membership in that family, you must live a righteous life. Through righteous living, you will allow the divine laws of God to guide your conduct and rule your life. Paramount among these principles is holiness and righteousness. Indeed, righteous living is a non-negotiable requirement for your continued membership in the family of God. Let us listen to the Psalmist:

Blessed is the man that
walketh not in the counsel of the
ungodly, nor standeth in the way of sinners,
nor sitteth in the seat of the scornful. But his delight
is in the law of the Lord; and in
his law doth he meditate
day and night. And he shall be like a tree planted by
the rivers of water, that bringeth forth his fruit in his

season; his leaf also shall not wither; and whatsoever
he doeth shall prosper. The ungodly are not so: but
are like the chaff which the wind driveth away.
Therefore the ungodly shall not
stand in the judgment,
nor sinners in the congregation of the righteous.
For the Lord knoweth the way of the righteous:
but the way of the ungodly shall perish..
(Psalm 1:1-6 KJV)

As the redeemed of the Lord, it is incumbent upon us to live a
holy and righteous life. We must thirst for this great attribute
of God because God wants us to be as holy and righteous as
He is. We must thirst for righteousness, as the Lord Jesus said
in the Book of Matthew:

**Blessed are they which do
hunger and thirst after righteousness:
for they shall be filled.** Matthew 5:6 (KJV)

As we look forward to the rapture and the second coming of our
Lord Jesus Christ, we must conduct ourselves every moment
of our lives in righteous manners that conform to the laws of
God and are pleasing to our heavenly Father. We must ensure
righteousness in our thoughts, feelings, speech, and behavior.
It is important for us to know that without righteousness, there
is no inheriting of eternal life with God in heaven.

**And thou shalt be blessed, for they cannot
Recompense thee, for thou shalt be recompensed.
at the resurrection of the just**.
Luke 14:14 (KJV)

LEARNING TO WALK WITH GOD LIKE ENOCH

God demands righteousness from us. If we want to walk with the righteous God, we must do what the laws of God require us to do. Our righteous Father wants us to be righteous in word and deed. Let's hear Apostle Paul speak on this matter:

God forbid: Yes, let God be true, but every man a liar; as it is written, That thou mightest be justified in thy sayings, and mightest overcome when thou art judged. Romans 3:4 (KJV)

Our righteousness must be total. In all our thoughts and imaginations, in everything we do, and in everything we say, we must be righteous. Indeed, we will give an account of all our utterances:

But I say unto you, That every idle word that men shall speak, they shall give account thereof in the day of judgment. For by thy words thou shalt be justified, and by thy words thou shalt be condemned. Matthew 12:36–37 (KJV)

In the same vein, our actions—what we do in all circumstances—actually show whether we are righteous or not. So, if we are really righteous, it must be seen; our righteousness must be palpable in all our deeds.

The Son of man came eating and drinking, and they say, Behold a man gluttonous, and a winebibber, a friend of publicans and sinners. But wisdom is justified of her children..'' Matthew 11:19, (KJV)

In Romans 3:4, the Apostle Paul has this counsel for us.

**God forbid: yea, let God be
true, but every man a liar; as
it is written, That thou mightest
be justified in thy sayings, and
mightest overcome when thou
art judged. Romans 3:4 (KJV)**

Out of His love for us, He saved us from eternal perdition. He pronounced us righteous and reconciled us to Himself. The righteous God ended the separation between Him and us—the progenies of Adam and Eve—that began in the Garden of Eden consequent upon the fall of Adam and Eve.

The Level Of Your Faith Determines Your Righteousness.

As children of God, we are expected to have absolute faith in our God. Indeed, a key benchmark for evaluating our righteousness is the level of our faith in God. We have a perfect exemplar in Abraham, who was adjudged righteous due to his strong faith in God.

**For what saith the scripture? Abraham
believed God, and it was counted unto him for
righteousness. Now to him, that work is
the reward not reckoned of grace but of debt.
But to him that worketh not, but believeth
on him that justifies the ungodly, his
Faith is counted for righteousness.**
Romans 4:3-5 (KJV)

As children of the Most High, our faith in His ability to save us from peril and our faith in His ability to meet us at the points of our needs must be unquestionable. It must be total. Our faith in God is required to prove ourselves righteous before Him. Without any iota of doubt, professing our belief in Christ Jesus is the basis of our salvation.

**For with the heart man believeth
unto righteousness; and with the mouth
confession is made unto salvation. For the
scripture saith, Whosoever believeth on
him shall not be ashamed
(Romans 10:10, KJV)**

When we have absolute faith in God's promises to us, even when they are yet to be fulfilled, then our utterances, our confessions, and our attitude, which are products of our strong faith in God, will make us considered righteous.

**Where is boasting then? It is excluded.
By what law? of works? Nay, but by the
law of faith. Therefore, we conclude that
A man is justified by faith without the
deeds of the law.** Romans 3:27–28 (KJV)

Nevertheless, in the words of the Apostle James, what you profess is not enough. A man or woman is adjudged righteous by the things that he does, not by his faith alone.

**You see, then, that a man is justified by
works, and not by faith only.**
James 2:24 (NKJV)

Therefore, my dear reader, you cannot be engaging in sinful acts and still want God to regard you as a righteous person in spite of your avowals. To be counted as a righteous person, you must steer clear of immoral acts. You must embrace holiness and do the right thing at all times.

> **Therefore, do not let sin reign**
> **in your mortal body; you should obey**
> **it in its lusts. 13 And do not present your**
> **members as instruments. of unrighteousness**
> **to sin, but present yourselves to God as being**
> **alive from the dead, and Your members as**
> **instruments of righteousness to God. 14 For**
> **sin shall not have dominion over you, for you are**
> **not under law but under grace.**
> **15 What then? Shall we**
> **sin because we are not under law but**
> **under grace? Certainly not!**
> Romans 6:12–15, New King James Version (NKJV)

My dear reader, it is a horrible thing to live an unrighteous life. Make no mistake about it: the reward of unrighteousness is the second death, eternal separation from God in hell, a place of eternal divine punishment. Let us hear the Apostle Paul.

For this reason, God gave them up to vile passions. Even their women exchanged the natural use of for what is against nature. [27] Likewise, the men, leaving the natural use of the woman, burned in their lust for one another, men with men committing what is shameful and receiving in themselves the penalty for their error, which was due. [28] And even as they did not like to retain God in *their* knowledge, God gave them over to

a debased mind, to do those things that are not fitting; being filled with all unrighteousness, sexual immorality, wickedness, covetousness, and maliciousness; full of envy, murder, strife, deceit, and evil-mindedness; They *are* whisperers, backbiters, haters of God, violent, proud, boasters, inventors of evil things, disobedient to parents, [31] undiscerning, untrustworthy, unloving, unforgiving, and unmerciful; [32] who, knowing the righteous judgment of God, that those who practice such things are deserving of death, not only do the same but also approve of those who practice them.

Romans 1:26-32 New King James Version (NKJV)

Dear reader, the ball is firmly in your court. Decide today to live for God by embracing God's counsel to you to live a righteous life so that you can live forever with Him in heaven. Apostle Paul is speaking to us again:

But now the righteousness of God without the law is manifested, being witnessed by the law and the prophets; even the righteousness of God which is by faith of Jesus Christ unto all and upon all those who believe, for there is no difference:

Romans 3:21–22, King James Version (KJV)

You can do it if you put your trust in the Lord Jesus Christ. He will help you to be righteous. Don't forget that your sins and mine, as well as those of the whole of humanity, have been imputed to him, as confirmed by Prophet Isaiah.

Surely he hath borne our griefs,
and carried our sorrows:
yet we did esteem him stricken,

smitten of God, and afflicted.
But he was wounded for our transgressions,
he was bruised for our iniquities:
the chastisement of our peace was upon him;
and with his stripes we are healed.
All we like sheep have gone astray;
we have turned everyone to his own way;
and the Lord hath laid on him the iniquity of us all
Isaiah 53:4-6, (KJV)

God imputes our sins to Christ, and He gives Christ's righteousness to us. Our sins are now bored by Jesus. In God's calculations, He debited Jesus Christ's account with our sins and the horrible punishment of death and went ahead to credit our own accounts with Jesus Christ's righteousness. No wonder the Apostle Paul, in his letter to the Christians in Corinth, declared thus:

[21] For He made Him who knew no sin *to be* sin.
for us, that we might become the righteousness
of God in him. 2 Corinthians 5:21 New King James
Version (NKJV)

CHAPTER SIX

BEING SURE OF
YOUR SALVATION

It is a good thing to choose to live for God. But that choice comes with a duty and a responsibility. It requires you to develop strong determination and an unwavering commitment to obeying and serving God with all your might and everything you have. It is about having a sense of commitment to the One who is your beginning and your end. Again, choosing to serve God is about fulfilling the key reason or purpose for which you are on earth. The essence of life is to discover the purpose of one's existence on planet Earth, and it is better if this discovery is made early enough so that one can achieve the reason why God created him or her, that is, the person's raison d'être on earth. In my own case, God was gracious enough to unfold His plan for my life very early through my mother. The Almighty revealed to her, a few days after I arrived on earth (the day of my christening ceremony), the reason why He sent me into this world. God did this because He wanted me to operate within His plan for my life right from my early years so that I could eventually achieve the destiny that He has given me.

God's major plan for my life was for me to serve Him as a minister of the gospel of His Son, Jesus Christ. But unfortunately, like in the case of many other people, I spurned God's plan for my life and turned down His invitation into His service. Nevertheless, God's matchless grace located me and rescued me. His mercy returned me to His original plan for my life and rescued me from the ruinous path of sin and worldliness that Satan diverted me into right from my early years. Oh yes!! God, in His mercy, rescued me from the bondage of sin and satanic enslavement by the enemy of my soul. God gave me the grace not only to be saved but also to accept His plan for my life, which is to serve Him, and I was able to answer His call into His service. Praise the Lord! Hallelujah!

Indeed, there is now joy in my heart. This joy of salvation is flowing from the inexhaustible fountain of life—Jesus Christ. The love of Christ now always fills my heart, and I now have a blessed assurance of hope of reigning in eternal life in heaven with my Christ, who redeemed me from nightclubbing, womanizing, alcohol, and other sundry vices that Satan used to entrap and enslave me.

My dearly beloved reader, there are some pertinent questions about the salvation of your souls that I would like to ask you. And I want you to answer these questions in your mind even as you are reading this book. The first question is: Are you really sure of your salvation? Or let me put it this way: "Are you really born again?" Okay, if your answer to these questions is yes, then I will further ask another probing question: "How committed are you to God, I mean your Creator?" Are you not one of the millions of people who go to church and attend church services and programs for reasons other than the salvation of their souls and are less concerned about life in eternity?

Indeed, my dear reader, the above questions are very germane to the issue of the salvation of your soul and where you will spend your eternity. Indeed, if the trumpet is sounded today, at this moment that you are reading this book, are you sure you will make heaven and be welcomed to the right hand of God where the saints, I mean the people whose sins have been forgiven and who have been cleansed by the redeeming blood of the Lamb of God, are gathered? My dear reader, do you have the assurance of making heaven when you die, or are you heading to hell, a place created and reserved by God for unrepentant sinners?

Unfortunately, millions of people who go to church today and who claim to be born-again cannot confidently give answers to the above questions in the affirmative. The simple reason for this is that they are still prevaricating on taking critical decisions that will ensure the salvation of their souls. They are yet to give the deserved attention to the issue of where they will spend their eternity when death closes their eyes here on earth. These people are still playing dangerous games with Satan, believing that they are smart. It is obvious that many Christians are not serious about God. Indeed, they do not know God, and God does not know them. They do not have any relationship with God, let alone engage in a life-long walk with Him. So, salvation of their souls is the least reason why they are in the church. Many of the Christians in this category do attend church's services and programs just because of what they can get from God. They are miracle collectors. They only use the church as a platform to socialize and access business opportunities. The achievement of their social and economic objectives is paramount in their minds, not the issue of the salvation of their souls. My dear reader, are you like them? If your honest answer is yes, please, I plead with you, in the name of God, to repent and have a change of heart so that you can fulfill the purpose for which your Creator sent you to the planet Earth.

Playing games with the Devil

Many years ago, I had a friend who claimed to be a child of God. This friend of mine was also serving in a church as a minister of God. He and I were close because he knew that I had a passion for soul-winning. However, I never knew he was one of the Christians playing games with the Devil. My friend was not committed to His Creator wholeheartedly. He had other reasons for being in the vineyard of God.

One day, my friend came up with the idea that we should leave our separate churches where we were worshipping and serving God to form a new church. Although I had some misgivings about his idea because I didn't want to leave my church, nevertheless, I decided to give him the benefit of the doubt and offer a helping hand to the new church project since I can still remain in my church and offer help to the new church. I felt that, after all, church is all about providing a platform for Christians to fellowship, grow in the Lord, and serve God. However, while offering my support to my friend's new church, I was conscious of the need to be careful about my association with the church. I was always praying to God for His guidance in regard to my activities in the new church so as not to go against His will.

Not too long after the church was formed, I began to discover, to my chagrin, the real reason why my friend formed the church. I began to notice some things that I knew were not right. Whenever I called the attention of my friend to these aberrations in the operations of the new church, his reply was usually that they were quite biblical. He always tells me to be patient and allow things to continue as they were, and that very soon, things will take normal shape. He was always quick to remind us of the fact that clergymen are supposed to eat from the altar, like the Levites in the Bible. He also usually tells me that "very soon, we too, like the Levites,will begin to eat from the altar. It then dawned on me that the reason why my friend established the church was to use it as a platform for his financial enrichment. I became very unhappy because I knew that it was dangerous to play games with the devil. I knew quite well that God would never be part of such a project. It was very appalling and disgusting to me that someone who is born-again will deliberately set up a church for the purpose of making money. I saw the whole idea as playing a game with Satan.

I detest to associate with people who love to exploit other people's religious fervor for money-making. Personal enrichment and aggrandizement weren't the reasons why I decided to be part of the church. I only wanted to contribute my own efforts to building a platform for people to congregate and serve God, not to join hands with some unscrupulous people to exploit others' faith for financial gains. But, alas, my friend was not concerned about winning souls into the kingdom of God. He was concerned about enriching himself through the church.

The Impact of Our Daily Walk With God

The basic proof of our salvation is the finished work done by Jesus Christ on the cross of the cavalry. This is the basis of the confidence that gives us the assurance that whenever Christ appears in the sky, as He will do one day, we will go home with Him. In other words, the assurances of our salvation are rooted in the work of redemption done by Jesus Christ on the cross of Calvary. Now, having been saved by the mercy and grace of God, we ought to proceed to the stage of working out our salvation every day by guarding our salvation jealously through running away from sin in order to be able to walk with God. We can do this by drawing strength and power on a day-to-day basis from the One who is only able to give that power. It is He who will empower us to work with Him. The impact of our daily walk with God will manifest in our spiritual development. This will be seen in our daily growth in the Lord up to the level of spiritual maturity, the development of spiritual capacity to obey God's Word, as well as having the fear of God in us. This is what will make us defer to Him in all our activities so as not to disobey God.

The finished work of Christ

The Bible assures us that God's promises are yes and amen. The Scripture tells us confidently concerning the fidelity of God's promises:

That by two immutable things, in which it was impossible for God to lie, we might have a strong consolation, who have fled for refuge to lay hold upon the hope set before us: Which hope do we have? as an anchor of the soul, both sure and steadfast, and which enters into that within the veil;
Hebrews 6:18–19, King James Version (KJV)

One of the surest bases for the assurance and security of our salvation, once we confess the Lord Jesus Christ as our Lord and personal Savior, is His finished work on the cross. Yes, the job of rescuing your soul and my soul from perdition in a place of eternal divine punishment was perfectly done by Jesus Christ. It is a perfect and finished job:

> **When Jesus, therefore, had**
> **received the vinegar, He said, It**
> **is finished, and he bowed his head**
> **and gave up the ghost.**
> **John 19:30, King James Version (KJV)**

If we indeed accept the finished work on the cross, then, instead of doubting, dear reader, you and I should be brimming with confidence! Jesus Christ's own word, which says, "*It is finished,* is an assurance that you and I, and everyone else who believes in Him, have the perfect and complete salvation given to us by God through His Son, Jesus Christ.

> **From henceforth expecting till his**
> **enemies be made his footstool. For by**
> **one offering he hath perfected forever**
> **them that are sanctified Whereof the Holy**
> **Ghost also is a witness to us: for after that**
> **he had said before (Hebrews 10:13-15 KJV)**

In effect, whenever Satan, the enemy of your salvation, comes to assail your mind with his arrows of doubt in order to deny you the joy of your salvation, all you need to do is remember the finished work on the cross.

> And **this is the testimony that God has given us.**
> **eternal life, and this life is in His Son. He who**
> **has the Son has a life; he who does not have the**
> **The Son of God does not have life. These things**
> **I have written to you who believe in the name of the**
> **Son of God, that you may know that you have eternal**
> **life, and that you may continue to believe in the name**
> **of the Son of God. (1 John 5:11–13, NKJV)**

Jesus tells us personally that He gives us eternal life, and nothing can take that away.

> My sheep hear my voice, and I know them, and
> They follow me, and I give them eternal life.
> and they shall never perish, nor shall any man
> pluck them out of my hand. My Father, who gave
> They are greater than all, and no man is able to
> pluck them out of my father's. I
> and my father are one.
> John 10:27-30 King James Version (KJV)

The assurance of our salvation in the Word of God

> And this is the testimony that God has given us.
> eternal life, and this life is in His Son. [12] He who has
> the Son has life; The he who does not have the Son
> of God does not have life. [13:] These
> things I have written
> to you who believe in the name
> of the Son of God, that
> you may know that you have eternal life, and You that
> You may *continue to* believe in the name of the Son.
> God. of God. (1 John 5:11–13, NKJV)

The objective truth in the Word of God is that if you believe that Jesus Christ is the Son of God and that He is your personal Lord and Saviour who died instead of you on the cross in order to pay the price for your sins, then you will be saved. Your salvation is a gift you received from God on account of your faith in His Son, whom He sent to implement His plan of redemption for mankind. Your salvation is not a product of your work of goodness or any good thing you have done. It is because you have accepted the Son that you believe in Him.

But as many as received him, to them gave He power. to become the sons of God, even to those who believe on his name, John 1:12, King James Version (KJV)

believe inDear reader, once you believe Jesus Christ and accept Him as your personal Lord and Saviour, then you have the Son (and you also have) life, which is salvation. The life (salvation) given to you is not temporary, but eternal. Indeed, God wants us to always have assurance of our salvation. We should not live our Christian lives wondering and worrying each day whether or not we are truly saved. That is why the Bible makes the plan of salvation so clear. Let's go to the scripture:

God so loved the world that he gave his
Only begotten Son, that whosoever believeth in him
should not perish but have everlasting life.
Believe in Jesus Christ.
John 3:16, King James Version (KJV)

Also, in Acts 16:31, Apostle Paul and Apostle Silas told the bewildered keeper of the prison, who sought to be saved, that all he needed to do was just believe in Jesus Christ, and his salvation was sure. Let's go to the Bible again:

So they said, "Believe in the Lord Jesus Christ,
and you will be saved, you and your household.
Acts 16:31, New King James Version (NKJV)

Also in the Book of Romans, the Apostle Paul's counsel to the early Christians further reinforced this fact:

That if thou shalt confess with thy mouth, the Lord Jesus, andshalt believe in thine heart that God hath raised him from the dead, thou shalt be saved.
Romans 10:9, King James Version (KJV)

At this juncture, dear reader, you need to do some self-examination and ask yourself some critical questions that are germane to your salvation. And mind you, there are only two possible answers—yes and no—to these questions. Now, let's go:

1. Have I repented of all my known and unknown sins?

2. Do I really believe that Jesus Christ died for me on the cross to pay the penalty for my sins and that He rose again from the dead on the third day?

3. Do I put my trust in Jesus Christ alone for my salvation?

If your answer to the above questions is yes, then you are saved. But if it is no or not sure, then there is a serious problem. Nevertheless, if your answer is no or not sure, I will urge you to quit vacillation and resolve today to identify with Jesus Christ and accept the finished work on the cross. If you can summon courage, defy Satan, the enemy of your soul, and stop toying with your eternity, you can rest assured that you will be saved. Now, listen to the Savior Himself as He speaks to you in this scripture:

**28 And I give unto them eternal life, and they shall
never perish, nor shall any man pluck them.
out of my hand. My Father, who gave them me,
is greater than all, and no man is able to pluck
them out of my father's hand.
"John 10:28–29, King James Version (KJV)**

The Road to Solid Assurance
of Your Salvation

1. Ask the Lord to reveal to you any known or unknown sin that exists in any area of your life and which you have yet to confess to the Lord. Make up your mind and cease dithering over these sins that the Lord has revealed to you.

2. Then take a step of courage by discarding those sins and resolving in your mind never to go back to them.

3. Become a Bible addict. You need to read your Bible daily, even voraciously, while you continue to commit your ways to the hands of God.

4. Regular prayer is non-negotiable. You need to develop a keen interest in prayer because that is a potent instrument for establishing and strengthening your relationship with God.

5. Put your trust in the Lord. Rely totally on Him for your daily instructions on how to conduct the affairs of your life because He loves you. If you do this, you can be sure that you will not regret your action.

6. And whenever Satan comes with his arrows of doubt, do not hesitate to use the power in the name of Jesus, the blood of Jesus, and the Word of God.

7. Always offer praise and thanksgiving to God for His mercy, goodness, blessings, and faithfulness. Do not allow Satan to let feelings rob you of the joy of God's salvation.

There is an incontrovertible truth we all must not forget. And that is the fact that salvation is a gift that God gave to us without our deserving it. We got it by His grace. And the simple reason this is so is because we have all sinned and flouted God's laws. And the inexorable outcome of our sin is spiritual death and eternal separation from our Creator, which began to manifest when God declared His judgment in the case of Satan (Satan) vs. Adam and Eve. We deserved this punishment because of Adam's and Eve's sins and our own sins too.

**For by grace are you saved through faith, and that
not of yourselves; it is the gift of God. Not of
works, lest any man should boast. We are
his workmanship, created in Christ Jesus unto
good works, which God hath before ordained that
We should walk in them.
Ephesians 2:8–10, King James Version (KJV)**

Now this is the greatest story of all time. God offered salvation to us, the progenies of Adam and Eve, from the consequences of our sins by sending His only begotten Son to die in our place so that anyone who believes in Jesus Christ would have had his punishment served by the Lamb of God who takes away the sins of the whole world.

The Lord Jesus Christ really loves us so much. He came to this world from heaven because of us. He lived a sinless life, went to the cross, died for our sin, and took the punishment that we deserved. Jesus Christ died on the third day. He rose from the grave on the third day and ascended to heaven, and He is now seated on the right hand of God, the Father.

My dear reader, do you accept and believe this story in your heart? If yes, and you can declare that Jesus Christ is not only the savior of the whole world but also your own personal Lord and Savior, then you will be saved from judgment and spend eternity with God in heaven.

CHAPTER SEVEN

HOLINESS: THE DAILY PURSUIT OF GENUINELY BORN-AGAIN CHRISTIANS

Sometime ago, I went with someone to buy some computers. After getting the computers, we put them in my cars, and we headed home. When I alighted from my car, this man left two of his laptop computers in my car's boot, and I didn't know that the computers were there. I never bothered to open the boot of the car when I got home. About two days later, when I opened the boot of my car, I found two laptop computers in a brown bag in the boot. I began to wonder where the laptop came from. It then dawned on me that they could have been part of the laptop computers I helped someone evacuate from where they were purchased some days earlier. I then decided to put a call through to the man and ask him if he really forgot two laptops in my car when he was alighting.

"Hello, did you leave two of your laptop computers in my booth", I asked the man.

"Are you just seeing them now?" he asked me.

"Yes, I just opened the boot of my car now, and I found two laptop computers there"

The man responded, "You know what? You're the real deal."

I then asked him what he meant by "you are the real deal". He now opened up and explained the motive for his actions. Unknown to me, the man deliberately left the two laptop computers in my car in order to test my integrity. He wanted to ascertain the authenticity of the information he had received about me.

"Someone told me that you are a Christian and that you can be trusted. I was also told that you are different from other Nigerians who have been found not to be honest and truthful and cannot be relied upon. And to confirm that, I decided to leave those laptop computers in your boot", he explained.

I was a bit surprised by his actions, and I just thanked him and ended the conversation. Indeed, God demands holiness and top-notch integrity from us as the redeemed of the Lord. He wants us to be as righteous as he is. By His very nature, God is holy. Everything about him is holy. Oh yes, our God is the only holy God. Listen to Apostle Peter speak:

**But as he who has called you holy, so be
Ye holy in all manner of conversation, because
It is written, Be ye holy, for I am holy.
(1 Peter 1:15 KJV).**

It is now very easy to understand why God demands holiness from all who want to associate with Him. Indeed, God desires a relationship with us human beings, but such a relationship must be built on holiness and righteousness.

The relationship between God and man began in the Garden of Eden after God created the first pair of human beings—Adam and Eve. As this relationship was blossoming, our arch enemy,

Satan, was planning to disrupt it. And soon, he came up with the strategy to destroy it through the instrumentality of sin— disobedience to God's holy law by Adam and Eve. But God never gave up on us because Satan's act and Adam's and Eve's betrayal never caught Him unaware. He simply reached out for his plan B, which he had designed beforehand. Through this plan, the loving God engineered a reconciliation of man to Himself through the death of His dear Son, Jesus Christ, who needed to die and shed His holy blood for the remission of our sins and our salvation.

My dear reader, having been saved by Jesus Christ's work of redemption on the cross, God is now requiring from you and I holiness and righteousness in everything we think, everything we say, and everything we do. Right on the Cross at Calvary where He died, Christ perfected the work of our spiritual amnesty, whereby we, who are dirty sinners, are declared righteous by virtue of Jesus Christ's righteousness. Our sins and guilt were transferred into Jesus Christ's account while Jesus Christ's righteousness and holiness were imputed to us. Hence, my dear beloved reader, all you need to do is to accept and enjoy the finished work of Jesus Christ on the cross of Calvary. Once you have taken that step of believing the Lord Jesus Christ and accepting Him as your Lord and Savior, you are automatically declared righteous and justified by God.

It is as simple as ABC. You are not required to do any work because Jesus Christ has done all the work for you. The only thing you need to do is believe in him and put your faith in him. It is your belief and faith that are required of you to access this finished work of redemption that Jesus has done for you. Now listen to the scriptures:

**Therefore, being justified by faith, we have
peace with God through our Lord Jesus
Christ: By whom also do we have access by faith?
into this grace wherein we stand and rejoice
in hope of the glory of God. And not only
So, but we glory in tribulations also: knowing
that tribulation worketh patience; and
patience, experience; and experience, hope:
And hope is not ashamed because the
The love of God is shed abroad in our hearts by the
Holy Ghost, which is given to us.
Romans 5:1 KJV**

After you have accepted Jesus Christ as your Lord and Saviour
and have appropriated the benefits of His obedience to God,
His father, and His death on the cross, you will need to go
further by deciding to shun all sins and dedicate yourself to
daily obedience to God's laws and commandments. You will
need to obey God's commandments, as stated in the Holy
Bible, and serve Him with everything you're doing. You will
need to make God your companion on the journey of life.
And to make God your companion in the journey of life, you
must be holy, because God cannot compromise holiness. It is
a major requirement you must have if you want to walk with
Him. Let's hear Apostle Peter again:

**Therefore, gird up the loins of your mind, be
sober, and hope to the end for the grace that is
to be brought unto you at the revelation of Jesus
Christ, as obedient children, do
not fashion yourselves.
According to the former lusts in your ignorance:
But as he who has called you holy, so be ye.**

**holy in all manner of conversation, because it is
written, Be ye holy, for I am holy.**
(1 Peter 1:13–16 KJV)

All those who want to walk with God as well as have a place of
eternal rest with Him in heaven must live a holy life. If indeed
you are truly saved, if your salvation is genuine, then you must
live a holy life.

What is holiness?

Holiness, in a simple sense, means to be separated from sin and
evil. Nevertheless, it is impossible to live a holy life without the
help of God. We, as human beings, do not have the capacity
to live a holy life. It is God, through His Holy Spirit, that can
empower us to live a holy life. Hence, dear reader, when God
fills you with His Holy Spirit, who will dwell in you, He will
fill you with the power to be holy. It is the Holy Spirit that
will enable you to overcome worldly temptations as well as
steer clear of sin.

**Ye are of God, little children,
and have overcome them: because
greater is he that is in you, than he that
is in the world. (1 John 4:4 KJV).**

In Galatians Chapter 5, Apostle Paul talked about walking in
the spirit and walking by the spirit. He stressed the importance
of walking in the spirit, as only then can we live a holy life and
be in tune with God. It is the Holy Spirit that will produce
Christ-like character and nature in us as we yield to Him

This I say then, Walk in the Spirit,
and ye shall not fulfil the lust
of the flesh. For the flesh lusteth against the Spirit,
and the Spirit against the flesh: and these are
contrary the one to the other: so that ye cannot
do the things that ye would. But if ye be led of the
Spirit, ye are not under the law. Now the works of
the flesh are manifest, which are these; Adultery,
fornication, uncleanness, lasciviousness, Idolatry,
witchcraft, hatred, variance, emulations, wrath, strife,
seditions, heresies, Envyings, murders, drunkenness,
revellings, and such like: of the
which I tell you before, as I
have also told you in time past, that
they which do such things
shall not inherit the kingdom of God. But the
fruit of the Spirit is love, joy, peace, longsuffering,
gentleness, goodness, faith, Meekness, temperance:
against such there is no law. And they that are
Christ's have crucified the flesh with the affections
and lusts. If we live in the Spirit, let us also walk
in the Spirit. Let us not be desirous of vain glory,
provoking one another, envying one another.
Galatians 5:16–26 (KJV)

Essential to holiness is obedience to the Word of God. We
can only live a holy life by being obedient to God's laws in all
areas of life.

As obedient children, not
fashioning yourselves according
to the former lusts in your ignorance:
But as he which hath called you is holy,

so be ye holy in all manner of conversation;
Because it is written, Be ye holy; for I am
holy.1 Peter 1:14–16 (KJV)

Knowing and obeying God's word is key to living a holy life.

"Therefore whosoever heareth
these sayings of mine, and doeth them,
I will liken him unto a wise man, which
built his house upon a rock:."
(Matthew 7:24 KJV)

As children of God who have accepted the work of redemption
done by Jesus Christ on the cross, we must not only be the
hearers of the word of God, but we must also be the doers of
the word.

But be ye doers of the word, and not hearers
only, deceiving your own selves. For if any be
a hearer of the word, and not a doer, he is like
unto a man beholding his natural face in a glass:
For he beholdeth himself, and goeth his way, and
straightway forgetteth what manner of man he
was. But whoso looketh into the perfect law of
liberty, and continueth therein, he being not a
forgetful hearer, but a doer of the work, this man
shall be blessed in his deed James 1:22 – 25 (KJV)

Satan will always intensely oppose the desire of every child of
God to put the word of God into practice. What we hear from
the preachers in the church, what we read on the internet or
read in the bible, must be internalized and put into practice.

Without us implementing what God says in His word, we are just mere jokers.

> **"Therefore whosoever heareth**
> **these sayings of mine, and doeth**
> **them, I will liken him unto a wise man,**
> **which built his house upon a rock:."**
> (Matthew 7:24 KJV).

In His valedictory prayers in John 17:17-20, the Lord Jesus Christ has this to say:

> **Sanctify them through thy truth; thy word is truth.**
> **As thou hast sent me into the**
> **world, even so have I also**
> **sent them into the world. And**
> **for their sakes, I sanctify**
> **myself, that they also might be**
> **sanctified through the truth.**
> **[20] Neither pray I for these alone, but for them also,**
> **shall believe in me through their word;**
> **John** 17:17–20 **(KJV)**

When we live in obedience to God, we are staying separate from evil.

When we keep God's words in our hearts (Psalm 119:11urgesRomans 12:1–2, which), we are helping ourselves to stay away from sin and live a holy life. It is when we have done this that we can heed the call of Apostle Paul in Romans12:1–2 which urge us to present our bodies to the Lord as living sacrifices to God.

EMMANUEL S. OMERE

I beseech you therefore, brethren, by the mercies
of God, that you present your
bodies as a living sacrifice,
holy, acceptable unto God, which is your reasonable
service. And be not conformed
to this world, but be ye
transformed by the renewing of
your mind, that you may
Prove what is good, acceptable, and perfect.
will of God (Romans 12:1–2 KJV).

The purpose of living a holy life is to glorify God and display
His nature to those around us.

Let your light so shine before men that they may
see your good works, and glorify your Father, which
is in heaven. Think not that I am
coming to destroy the law,
or the prophets: I am not come
to destroy, but to fulfill.
18 For verily, I say unto you, Till
heaven and earth pass,
One jot or one tittle shall, in no
wise, pass from the law.
all be fulfilled. Whoever therefore shall break one of
these least commandments, and shall teach men so, he
shall be called the least in the kingdom of heaven, but
Whoever shall do and teach them, the same shall be
called great in the kingdom of heaven.
20 For I say unto you, That except your righteousness
shall exceed the righteousness of
the scribes and Pharisees,
You shall, in no case, enter the kingdom of heaven.

82

Matthew Mathew 5:16–20 (KJV)

My dear reader, there is no contesting the fact that holiness within and without and living a righteous life are non-negotiable in our quest to please God. Living a life of obedience to God's laws is the veritable way to escape from sin.

Knowing this, our old man is crucified with him, that the body of sin might be destroyed, that Henceforth, we should not serve sin. living in true freedom from the bondage of sin Romans 6:6 (KJV)

Be Dead to Sin

Now, after all said and done, we must admit that living a holy life is not an easy task. It is more of a herculean task for a person who relies on his or her own abilities. We must know that our arch-enemy, Satan, is always ready to obstruct our path to holiness whenever we choose to travel on that road. Hence, we must rely totally on the Holy Spirit to help us be holy in our thoughts, utterances, and actions.

Then he answered and spoke to me, saying, This This is the word of the Lord to Zerubbabel, saying, Not by might nor by power, but by my spirit, saith the Lord of hosts. Who art thou, O great mountain? Before Zerubbabel thou shalt become a plain, and he shall

**bring forth the headstone thereof
with shouting, crying,
Grace, grace unto it**.
Zechariah 4:6–9 (KJV)

It therefore goes without saying that we must draw our strength from the counsel given to us by the Apostle Paul:

**[11] Likewise, reckon ye also yourselves to be dead.
indeed unto sin, but alive unto God through Jesus
Christ is our Lord. Let not sin therefore reign in your
mortal body, that you should obey
it in the lusts thereof.
Neither yield you your members as instruments of
unrighteousness unto sin, but yield yourselves unto
God, as those that are alive from the dead, and
your members as instruments of righteousness unto
God**. Romans 6:11–13 (KJV)

Thus, anytime Satan comes with temptation for us to commit sin, we must remember that, as someone who was baptized into Jesus Christ's death, we should tell the enemy of our soul that "I am dead to sin; I cannot do that anymore. I am a new creature in Christ! I now live a new life driven by the law of God and the virtue of holiness.

In case you stumble...

It is important for us to know that even as children of God who are born-again, we are not infallible. Our perfection is only in Jesus Christ. As long as we still remain in our mortal bodies, we are susceptible to sin. That is why we should be on guard against sin and temptation 24 hours a day. Nevertheless, when we sometimes run foul of the laws of God, we must not allow ourselves to be depressed. As the redeemed of the Lord, at that moment, when the Holy Spirit has convicted us of our sin, we need to pick ourselves up and run to our advocate, Jesus Christ.

My little children, these things I write to you,

that you sin not. And if any man sins, we have an advocate with the Father, Jesus Christ the righteous: 2 And he is the propitiation for our sins, and not for ours only, but also for the sins of the whole world. 1 John 2:1-2 (KJV)

God will never abandon us when we make mistakes. His love and grace for us will still persist. *"There is now no condemnation for those who are in Christ Jesus."* God's grace doesn't go away when we make mistakes. Nevertheless, we must pursue holiness at all times. A pursuit of holiness is an earnest desire to walk with God. As we endeavor to live a holy life, God Himself will continue to draw us nearer to Himself. Our life of holiness will bring glory to God. When we live holy lives, we reflect God's character to the world. We become lights in a dark world that lead the way to the Savior.

CHAPTER EIGHT

BE READY TO GIVE ACCOUNT TO YOUR CREATOR

"For we must all appear before the judgment seat of Christ that each one may be recompensed for his deeds in the body, according to what he has done, whether good or bad."(2Corinthians 5:10 KJ)

It has been divinely decreed by God that every human being that has ever lived on planet Earth must give an account of his or her sojourn on earth after the end of our tour of duty on earth. All the wicked people (the unrepentant sinners), who rejected Christ while they were on the planet Earth, will on that day go to a place of eternal divine punishment, God's prison yard for Satan and his cohorts. The saved, born-again Christians who have received Christ as their Lord and Saviour will go to heaven. While the saints (the people of God) will appear before the Judgment Seat of Christ to be rewarded according to their works for the Kingdom of God on earth, the impenitent sinners will appear before the White Throne Judgement of God to receive their sentences of eternal punishment in a place of eternal divine punishment. And that is their eternal, irreversible judgment.

It is an incontrovertible fact that everyone who is born into this world, whether black or white, male or female, rich or poor, young or old, slave or free-born, is certainly accountable to

LEARNING TO WALK WITH GOD LIKE ENOCH

Jehovah God. It is important to know that God is watching us, keeping His eyes on every thought in our minds, every word that comes out of our mouths, and every action we take in our daily lives. We must know that we shall surely give account of all our thoughts, actions, and utterances that contravene the laws of God. And it is also pertinent for us to know that due divine punishment awaits us for every infraction of the laws of the Almighty God, unless we embrace the services of the Divine Advocate God has chosen to plead on our behalf, the Lord Jesus Christ.

The Lord Jesus Christ indeed warned the Jews and alerted them to the fact that they needed to be careful in their conduct because of the Day of Personal Accountability before God. Christ told them that they would be held accountable for every foul word that came out of their mouths on the Day of Accountability. Hear what the Lord says in the Book of Matthew:

But I say unto you, That every idle word that men shall speak, they shall give account thereof in the day of judgment. For by thy words thou shalt be justified, and by thy words, thou shalt be condemned. (Mathew 12:36-37 KJV).

The question you may ask is, "Will anyone be able to escape unscathed on that day?" Well, the Bible told us that on this issue, humanity is in a dire strait and that the only way out for any person who wants to be justified on that day is to be wise and, without hesitation, believe in and accept the Lordship of Jesus Christ. The Lord is the One who will be the Advocate of those who believe in Him on that day, because we are not qualified to make a case for ourselves since, right from the Garden of Eden, we have been guilty as charged. Let us see what the Bible tells us about our precarious situation on this matter:

As it is written, there is none righteous, no.
not one: There is none that understands, there
is none that seeketh after God. They are all gone.
out of the way, they have together become
unprofitable; there is none that does good, no,
not one. (Romans 3:12 KJV)

Oh yes, my dear reader, the only way out for you is to accept Jesus Christ as your Lord and Saviour so that you can be able to give a good and praiseworthy account on that day. It is inevitable for all human beings to account for their lives. And the wise ones among men will do well by engaging the services of the only competent advocate who will plead on their behalf on that day. Why do I need an advocate, you may ask? The simple reason is that every human being on earth has inherited the sins of Adam and Eve. Our predicament became compounded by our own personal transgressions against the laws of God. But because of His love for us, for Him to be able to redeem us, and for the demands of His just law, which required death for sinners to be met, God the Father, the owner of the universe, chose to make His Son, Jesus Christ, the divine sacrificial lamb for you, me, and the rest of humanity. Hence the Lord declared in the Book of John:

That all men should honour the
Son, even as they honour the Father.
He that honoureth not the Son honoureth
not the Father which hath sent him. Verily, verily,
I say unto you, He that heareth
my word, and believeth

**on him that sent me, hath
everlasting life, and shall not
come into condemnation; but is
passed from death unto
life.. (John 5:23-24 KJV)**

Consequently, all your sins, my own sins, and the sins of the
rest of the world, as well as the guilt arising from all our
transgressions and our due punishment, have been borne by
the Saviour since He died on the cross. Hence, on the Day of
Accountability, the work of redemption done for humanity
on the cross by Jesus Christ, the Messiah, will speak for those
who believe in and accept Him as their savior and Lord. But
the reverse will be the case for those who refuse to believe
and accept Jesus Christ as their Lord and Saviour before death
closes their eyes. This is because they have no part in the work
of redemption on the cross, and they cannot enjoy the reprieve
that will come the way of the saints of God who have been
washed and redeemed by the precious blood of the Divine
Lamb of God.

Dear reader, Are you among this multitude of people who
are still vacillating and toying with their eternity? Remember
that those who are still dithering on the critical issue of the
salvation of their souls are indeed living dangerously because
death can come at any time. When they find themselves on
the other side of the Great Divide, they will have no excuse
for their punishment because a grand offer of salvation was
made to them by God, but they rejected it. They will therefore
give account to God for their refusal to accept God's offer of
salvation as well as all their transgressions against the laws of
God. They will be held accountable for their sinful lives and
all the bad choices they made on earth. But then, they will be

alone; there will be no advocate for them because they have rejected the only one who can make a case for them while they were still on earth.

Nevertheless, God never wanted anyone to be condemned on the Last Day. It is not the joy of God for any human being to go to a place of eternal divine punishment, the place of eternal suffering and gnashing of teeth. Indeed, hell, God's place of eternal divine punishment, was created for Satan and other fallen angels. It was not meant for mankind. And to avert sending us there, on account of the sins of our first parents, Adam and Eve, and our own personal sins, God had to activate His plan of salvation and make His dear Son, Jesus Christ, the propitiation for the sins of the whole world. Let's hear Apostle John speak on this matter:

**My little children, these things write
I unto you, that ye sin not. And if any
man sin, we have an advocate with the
Father, Jesus Christ the righteous: And
he is the propitiation for our sins: and not
for ours only, but also for the sins of the
whole world. (1 John 2:1-2 KJV)**

In the Book of John, the Bible further expounded this agape love shown by God to the rebellious human race. The Bible says:

**God so loved the world that he gave his only
begotten Son, that whosoever believeth in him should
not perish, but have everlasting life. For God sent not
his Son into the world to condemn the world, but**

**that the world through him might be saved.
(John 3:16 KJV)**

Unfortunately, it is this great, unfeigned love that billions of people are rejecting today. They are allowing themselves to be deceived by Satan, the arch enemy of their souls, who wants them to join him in a place of eternal divine punishment. Hence, dear reader, if you are yet to accept Jesus Christ as your advocate on the Day of Accountability, you are surely in a state of jeopardy. You need to get out of the trap of Satan and embrace God's offer of free salvation to all sinners.

**But God commendeth his love
toward us, in that, while we were
yet sinners, Christ died for us. Much
more then, being now justified by his
blood, we shall be saved from wrath through
him. For if, when we were enemies, we were
reconciled to God by the death of his Son,
much more, being reconciled, we shall be
saved by his life. (Romans 5:8-11 KJV)**

It is therefore an awe-inspiring spectacle to be contemplated, for you to reject God's offer of Free salvation here on earth and then to find yourself standing before your Creator, on the Day of accountability, to account for your numerous misdeeds here on earth without an advocate. Believe it or not, there will be no room for advocacy or pleading in front of the White Throne Judgment of God. not come into condemnation; but is passed from death unto life. The necessary advocacy and pleadings for sinners have been done by Jesus Christ on the cross. That is why all those who believe in **Him "shall not come into condemnation; but is passed from death unto** life" **(John 5:24)** No matter how eloquent and brilliant you are, you cannot escape punishment on that day for all your transgressions unless you have Jesus. All your wrongdoings that you think are hidden or unknown to God are indeed right there recorded in His books, both in audio and video format. Indeed, it is a frightening situation! And whether we like it or not, both the saved Christians and the impenitent sinners will be judged. However, the judgment of the saints of God is to enable them to appear at the judgment seat of Christ to receive rewards for their works on earth, while on the other hand, the impenitent sinners will have to stand before the Great White Throne Judgment of God to get their sentences for their due punishment in hell, the place of eternal divine punishment created by God.

**"And, behold, I come quickly, and my reward is
with me, to give every man according to
His work shall be" (Rev. 22:12 KJV).**

No Hiding Place Before God

The Almighty God is the creator of heaven and earth. The Lord knows everything about us, right from the moment we were born into this world up to the very second we depart the planet Earth. He also monitors all our daily activities. All our thoughts, utterances, and actions are being recorded by Him. So, there is no escaping his roving eyes! Let's listen to God's warning through Prophet Jeremiah:

**For mine eyes are upon all their ways:
they are not hid from my face, neither is
their iniquity hid from mine eyes..
(Jeremiah 16:17 KJV)**

In the Book of Second Chronicles, the Bible declares that everything we do on earth is right before God. In rebuking King Asa for seeking help from a foreign land, instead of putting his trust in Jehovah God, God told the king through a seer that all the thoughts and plans of the king are known to Him even before the king contemplates his actions:

> **For the eyes of the Lord run to**
> **and fro throughout the whole earth,**
> **to shew himself strong in the behalf of**
> **them whose heart is perfect toward him.**
> **Herein thou hast done foolishly: therefore**
> **from henceforth thou shalt have wars.**
> **(2 Chronicles 16:9 KJV)**

Job, even in his distress, was careful not to offend God because, according to him, God was monitoring him and knew everything about the situation he was in. Let's hear Job:

> **Doth not he see my ways,**
> **and count all my steps?**
> **(Job 31:4 KJV)**

In the Book of Hebrews, the Bible declares:

> **Neither is there any creature**
> **that is not manifest in his sight:**
> **but all things are naked and opened**
> **unto the eyes of him with whom we have**
> **to do.** (Hebrews 4:13 KJV).

We will therefore be deceiving ourselves if we think either God is unaware of all the atrocities we are committing here on earth or that He does not care about them, or if we think that all our wicked acts will go unpunished despite the fact that we have rejected God's offer of mercy, which is Jesus Christ. The Lord sees everything we are doing, and He will hold us accountable for all our thoughts, utterances, and actions. Each and every one of those who spurned God's offer of salvation will bear the repercussions of their acts. God affirmed this fact in the Book of Ezekiel. He declared:

> **"Yet say ye, Why? doth not the
> son bear the iniquity of the father?
> When the son hath done that which is
> lawful and right, and hath kept all my statutes,
> and hath done them, he shall surely live. The soul
> that sinneth, it shall die. The son shall not bear
> the iniquity of the father, neither shall the father
> bear the iniquity of the son: the righteousness
> of the righteous shall be upon him, and the
> wickedness of the wicked shall be upon
> him. (Ezekiel 18:19–20 KJV).**

Indeed, the way we live our lives here on planet Earth matters a lot. It is the spiritual quality of the life we lived here on earth and our obedience to the commandments of God that will determine whether we will pass from death to life, as the Lord Jesus declared in the Scriptures, or whether we will move from judgment to condemnation. For those who are yet to belong to God's commonwealth of favor and mercy, facilitated by the birth, death, and resurrection of Jesus Christ, there is so much work for them to do. They need to make hay while the sun is still shining. When the gospel is preached to us, we are faced with two options: believe it by faith or reject it. Those who believe and accept the message of salvation in the gospel are saved by God's grace, the unmerited favor, mercy, and love that God is still showing to all mankind. Those who are negligent and opt to discountenance this God's free gift of salvation will regrettably and surely end in perdition, God's divinely decreed punishment and punishment for all unrepentant sinners in a place of eternal divine punishment and eternal torments.

The Bible mentioned many deeds that those who rejected Jesus Christ here on earth will account for on the Day of Accountability. According to the Apostle Paul in his letter to early Christians in Galatia, "such people shall not inherit the kingdom of God". Let's listen to Paul:

> **Now the works of the flesh
> are manifest, which are these;
> Adultery, fornication, uncleanness,
> lasciviousness, Idolatry, witchcraft,
> hatred, variance, emulations, wrath,
> strife, seditions, heresies, Envyings,
> murders, drunkenness, revellings, and
> such like: of the which I tell you before,
> as I have also told you in time past, that
> they which do such things shall not
> inherit the kingdom of God.
> (Galatians 5:19–21 KJV).**

Anyone who still indulges in the above nefarious activities certainly does not know Jesus Christ. Even if such a fellow claims to be a Christian, it is palpably clear that he or she is wallowing in self-delusion and that such a fellow does not know Christ. It is therefore imperative for all those who have confessed Jesus Christ as their Lord and Savior to remain focused and jealously guard their salvation. They need to allow

God to work on their lives so that they can become transformed into those holy people who will daily seek to obey and please God. Our transformation by the Holy Spirit is crucial. This will help us to grow spiritually daily and strive to please God in all our ways. We must therefore be preoccupied every day as believers with the goal of getting closer to God through prayers and studying the Word of God so that we can become what He desires us to be. We must put our conviction and belief into action. Yes, as Apostle Paul told us, we must daily work out our salvation.

> **Wherefore, my beloved, as
> ye have always obeyed, not
> as in my presence only, but now
> much more in my absence, work out
> your own salvation with fear and
> trembling. For it is God which worketh
> in you both to will and to do of his good
> pleasure. (Philippians 2:12-13 KJV)**

Irrespective of the challenges that may come our way, because these challenges will surely come, we must never be daunted. Rather, we must rely on His unfailing grace, remain focused on living a holy life, and indeed be righteousness in all our undertakings, as the Bible counseled us:

> **Follow peace with all men,
> and holiness, without which no
> man shall see the Lord: Looking diligently
> lest any man fail of the grace of God; lest
> any root of bitterness springing up trouble you,**

and thereby many be defiled; Lest there be any fornicator, or profane person, as Esau, who for one morsel of meat sold his birthright.

(Hebrew 12:14–15 KJV).

CHAPTER NINE

TRANSITING TO THE GREAT BEYOND

Across the world, several thousand people close their eyes and bid the planet Earth good-bye. With a last silent or deep breath, they cross into eternity and join the so-called Great Beyond. The big question has always been, "What happens to them thereafter?" The Scriptures provide a profound answer to that question:

> **And as it is appointed unto men once**
> **to die, but after this, the judgment**
> **(Hebrew 9:27 KJV)**

The moment a person dies, the soul of that person exits the body, which remains on earth. While the body goes back to the earth where it came from, the soul goes back to God, according to the Bible in Ecclesiastes:

> **Then shall the dust return to the earth as it was:**
> **and the spirit shall return unto God, who gave it.**
> **(Ecclesiastes 12:17 KJV)**

For the saints (those the Bible called the people of God who accepted Jesus Christ as their Lord and personal Saviour and who obeyed His commandments while on earth), are carried by the angels into the presence of the Lord just as those who spurned God's offer of FREE salvation, through faith in the death and resurrection of Jesus Christ, God's holy sacrificial lamb for the sins of humanity, take their place as their place of abode while awaiting the judgment day, as we read in the case of Lazarus and the rich man in the Book of Luke:

"And in hell he lifted up his eyes, being in torment, and seeth Abraham afar off, and Lazarus in his bosom. And he cried and said, Father Abraham, Have mercy on me and send Lazarus, that he may dip the tip of his finger in water, and cool my tongue, for I am tormented in this flame. But Abraham said, Son, remember that thou in thy lifetime receivedst thy good things, and likewise, Lazarus evil things, but now he is comforted, and thou art tormented. And beside all this, between us and you, there is a great gulf fixed: so that they would pass from hence to You cannot; neither can they pass to us; that would come from thence. (Luke 16:23–27 KJV)

However, God, in His infinite wisdom, never planned that man should die. We human beings were not created to die! On the sixth day of His work of creation, God created Adam, the progenitor of the human race. Thereafter, the Lord provided a helpmate for him, Eve, his wife. God also provided a wonderful home for them, a home stocked with foods of all kinds as well as the physical and spiritual comfort the couple needed. The icing on the cake for them was that God created them as beings that were to live perpetually.

Nonetheless, God followed up His benevolent acts with a caveat: "You may surely eat of every tree of the garden, but of the tree of the knowledge of good and evil you shall not eat, for in the day that you eat of it you shall surely die." (Genesis 2:15-17).

Unfortunately, God's kind acts of compassion were rewarded with rebellion. In spite of God's warning, which they clearly understood, Adam and Eve went on to rebel against God. Consequently, they brought sin into the world and the due punishment of the loss of eternal life and death that followed. Their progenies, the rest of the human race, inexorably inherited sin as well as the divine punishment of physical and spiritual death from their rebellious parents, Adam and Eve. And so has it been since then. However, owing to His undying love for humanity, God wanted to reconcile with us. He wanted to remove the yoke of eternal punishment from man. Thus, He initiated the process of reconciliation between Himself and the human race by activating His already-made plan of salvation for the human race. This He did by sending His Son, Jesus Christ, to this world, the Messiah, who knew no sin but was made sin in order for Him to suffer the punishment due to humanity as God's justice demanded.

Jesus Christ eventually died in the place of the whole human race in order for us to be redeemed through His death and resurrection. Through this medium, God perfected the reconciliation process, thereby restoring the hitherto rebellious human race to the position we lost in Eden consequent upon the sin of Adam and Eve. Let's listen to the confirmation of this in the Apostle Paul's letter to the early Christians in the City of Corinth:

> To wit, that God was in Christ,
> reconciling the world unto himself,
> not imputing their trespasses unto them;
> and hath committed unto us the word of
> reconciliation. Now then we are ambassadors
> for Christ, as though God did beseech you by
> us: we pray you in Christ's stead, be ye reconciled
> to God. For he hath made him to be sin for us, who
> knew no sin; that we might be made the righteousness
> of God in him.. (2 Corinthians 5: 19-21 KJV)

God demonstrated His love for mankind via His package of salvation, as recorded in the Book of John:

> "For God so loved the world, that
> he gave his only begotten Son, that
> whosoever believeth in him should not perish,
> but have everlasting life. For God sent not his Son
> into the world to condemn the
> world; but that the world
> through him might be saved. He that
> believeth on him is not condemned: but he
> that believeth not is condemned already,
> because he hath not believed in the name of the only
> begotten
> Son of God. And this is the
> condemnation, that light is come
> into the world, and men loved darkness rather
> than light, because their deeds were evil. For
> every one that doeth evil hateth the light, neither
> cometh to the light, lest his deeds should be
> reproved. But he that doeth truth cometh to the

light, that his deeds may be made manifest, that they are wrought in God. (John 3: 16–21KJV)

Hence, God's offer of salvation is free, and it is available to everyone. But unfortunately, not everyone is embracing it. And as the Scriptures say, those who rebuffed God's offer are in danger of incurring God's wrath, just like the rich man in the Lazarus story, while reward for obedience and faith in God awaits those who believed Jesus Christ and accepted Him like Lazarus did. In his speech to the people of Athens at Areopagus, the Apostle Paul confirmed this:

> **And the times of this ignorance**
> **God winked at; but now commandeth**
> **all men everywhere to repent: Because**
> **he hath appointed a day, in the which**
> **he will judge the world in righteousness**
> **by that man whom he hath ordained; whereof**
> **he hath given assurance unto all men, in that he**
> **hath raised him from the dead.** (Acts 17:30-31 KJV).

Judgment Day is the day of final and eternal judgment by God. It is the day that the Almighty has set aside to punish people who rejected Jesus Christ and reward those who put their faith in Him. Consequently, for the unrepentant sinners, the judgment day is certainly "the great day of his wrath," according to the Book of Revelation, chapter 6, verse 7, and indeed, "the day of God's wrath, when his righteous judgment will be revealed" against those who refused God's offer of reconciliation and salvation, according to the Apostle Paul in Romans 2:5.

Judgment Day Is Inevitable, It Can't Be Avoided

The first and most important thing to understand about the final judgment is that it can't be avoided. Again, let's go back to the Book of Hebrews, where the Bible declares:

And as it is appointed unto men once to die, but after this the judgment: (Hebrews 9:27 KJV)

A divine and unavoidable appointment given by God awaits all humanity. A fearful day of accountability for all men and women is in the offing. In his vision of Patmos Island, Apostle John gave us a clear perspective on this Day of Judgment:

And I saw a great white throne, and him that sat on it, from whose face the earth and the heaven fled away; and there was found no place for them. And I saw the dead, small and great, stand before God; and the books were opened: and another book was opened, which is the book of life: and the dead were judged out of those things which were written in the books, according to their works. (Revelation 20:11–12 KJV).

After we die here on earth, those choices we made in every situation we found ourselves in while we were still on this side of the Great Divide will become the basis of the decisions God will take concerning each and every one of us. For those who discountenanced God's love and unmerited favor and mercy by refusing to do away with sinful lives and embrace righteousness, they will surely go to the place of eternal divine punishment created and reserved for sinners.

And those who believe in God and embrace righteous and holy living will go to heaven. In the words of Apostle Paul, the believers' case will just be like being **"absent from the body and to be present with the Lord." (2Corinthians 5:8).** For believers in Jesus Christ who accept Him as their personal Lord and Saviour, death even opens the door to a better life for them because, as Paul puts it, "to live is Christ, and to die is gain". (Philippians 1:21), and to die is much better (Philippians 1:23).

CHAPTER TEN

JESUS CHRIST: GOD'S ROADMAP TO ETERNITY IN HEAVEN

T he Merriam-webster dictionary defines a road map as: "a map showing roads especially for automobile travel." It also explained further that a roadmap can be a "detailed plan that will guide progress toward a goal" (www.merriam-webster.com/dictionary).

If we are to expand the meaning of this word further, according to *www.productplan.com,* we can simply describe a roadmap as a "strategic plan that defines a goal or desired outcome, and includes the major steps or milestones needed to reach it".

Eternity Is A Must

In the sweat of thy face
shalt thou eat bread, till thou
return unto the ground; for out
of it wast thou taken: for dust thou
art, and unto dust shalt thou return.
(Genesis 3:19 KJV)

By the above divine decree made by God while adjudicating in the case of humanity versus Satan in the Garden of Eden, man lost the chance to live forever on earth. The humanity was sentenced to compulsory physical death on earth. We must die physically and be buried here on earth. But that is not the end of the story because the soul of man will not be exterminated at death. It still continues to live in an endless dispensation called eternity. Yes, eternity is awaiting every soul.

The soul of man, upon cessation of life on earth, must continue to live eternally, either in heaven or hell, the place of eternal divine punishment created and reserved for sinners. Fire. So, right from day one of a child's birth, his or her journey to eternity has begun. Every human being on earth is a traveler to the eternity.

The Journey Called Eternity

Every traveler embarking on a journey, long or short-distance, needs a map to ensure that he or she arrives at the desired destination. This is also the case in the journey to eternity which every man or woman, boy or girl on planet earth must undertake. The Bible clearly teaches that this world is not our home. Indeed, the scripture makes it clear to us that everyone on earth is a sojourner. We didn't originate from here, we are sent here by the Almighty God and whether we like it or not, upon the completion of our tour of duty, we must return home. We must exit this present world because one day, it would be destroyed by God.

In God's original plan, we were not supposed to die, but Satan, through the sin of Adam and Eve changed that and we lost the grace to live forever. Hence it has become a necessity for us to exit the world and die physically after our appointed time to live on earth.

**In the sweat of thy face
shalt thou eat bread, till thou
return unto the ground; for out
of it wast thou taken: for dust thou
art, and unto dust shalt thou return.**
(Genesis 3:19 KJV)

Consequent upon the sin of Adam and Eve, we were to spend eternity in torments in the place of eternal divine punishment created and reserved for sinners. But God in His infinite mercy gave us a second chance through His redemptive plan designed to save us from sin and its commensurate punishment which is both physical and spiritual death as well as eternal separation from God.

Let us listen to Apostle Paul:

**But God commendeth his love toward us, in
that, while we were yet sinners, Christ died for us.
(Romans 5:8 KJV)**

God's plan of redemption was executed by Him via the sending of Jesus Christ, His only Son, to this world to suffer the just consequences of the sin of Adam and Eve and the sins of we the progenies of this first pair of human beings, which is spiritual death. And now there is a decree by God compelling everyone to accept His redemptive plan or be punished for rejecting it.

**That whosoever believeth in him should not perish,
but have eternal life. For God so loved the world, that
he gave his only begotten Son,
that whosoever believeth
in him should not perish, but have everlasting life. For**

God sent not his Son into the world to condemn the world; but that the world through him might be saved. He that believeth on him is not condemned: but he that believeth not is condemned already, because he hath not believed in the name of the only begotten Son of God. (John 3:15-18 KJV)

The acceptance of God's redemptive plan will result in a life of bliss in paradise in eternity while the rejection of the redemptive plan is a sentence to eternal banishment from our original home—heaven-- to Hell, the place of eternal divine punishment created and reserved for sinners. the BIG jail God has prepared for those who rejected His plan of redemption. So, either way, whether we accept God's redemptive plan or reject it, it is of necessity for us to go to eternity and meet our reward which is waiting for us there. Apostle once again speaks:

And as it is appointed unto men once to die, but after this the judgment: (Hebrews 9:27 KJV)

Our home is in heaven where we will live in the eternity. In the word of Apostle Peter, we are sojourners and pilgrims here on the earth. Our home is in heaven where God lives. God wants every human being He has created to come and live with Him in heaven after our sojourn here on planet earth. In the present world, we are foreigners or sojourners. We are on journey into eternity.

And if ye call on the Father , who without respect of persons

**judgeth according to every man's
work, pass the time of your
sojourning here in fear:.**
(1 Peter 1:17 KJV)

But there are conditions attached to this open invitation to
Paradise by God. Let us hear Apostle Peter once again:

**Dearly beloved, I beseech you
as strangers and pilgrims, abstain
from fleshly lusts, which war against
the soul; Having your conversation
honest among the Gentiles: that,
whereas they speak against you
as evildoers, they may by your
good works, which they shall
behold, glorify God in the
day of visitation.**
(1 Peter 2:11-12 KJV)

Apostle John further reinforces the point that this world is not
our home and that one day the world will cease to exist:

**And the world passeth
away, and the lust thereof:
but he that doeth the will of
God abideth forever.**
(1 John 2:17 KJV)

In his letter to Christians in Philippi, Apostle Paul stressed the
fact that we do not belong here; we are not world citizens, we
are heavenly citizens.

> **For our conversation**
> **(citizenship emphasis mine) is**
> **In heaven; from whence also we**
> **look for the Saviour, the Lord**
> **Jesus Christ: Who shall change**
> **our vile body, that it may be fashioned**
> **like unto his glorious body, according**
> **to the working whereby he is able even**
> **to subdue all things unto himself.**
> Phil. 3:20-21 KJV

Indeed, our real home is in heaven the heavenly city God has prepared for those who accept His only begotten Son, Jesus Christ. The Lord Jesus Christ spoke about our eternal home:

> **In my Father's house are many mansions: if it**
> **were not so, I would have told you. I go to**
> **prepare a place for you. And if I go and prepare a**
> **place for you, I will come again, and receive you**
> **unto myself; that where I am, there ye may be also.**
> **And whither I go ye know, and the way ye know.**
> John 14:2-4 King James Version (KJV)

The Safe Road To Eternity

Just as people do not randomly choose roads when they are travelling, everyone embarking on the journey to eternity must consciously and carefully choose the route that will take him or her to eternity. In our own case here, there are two possible roads:

(a) The Broad Way
(b) The Narrow Way

A large multitude of people are traveling on the Broad Way. The Lord Jesus Christ warned us against travelling on the Broad Way:

Enter by the narrow gate; for wide is the gate and broad is the way that leads to destruction, and there are many who go in by it. [a]Because narrow is the gate and [b]difficult is the way which leads to life, and there are few who find it
Matthew 7:13-14 New King James Version (NKJV)

The Broad Way is a dangerous route to eternity only the Narrow Way is safe. But unfortunately, as dangerous as the Broad Way is, a huge number of people prefer to travel on this perilous route. The Almighty God knew the journey to eternity is a must for every human being. God is also aware of the fact that there are just two routes to the eternity: one is good the other is dreadful. But God has a solution which He has designed even before He laid the foundation of the earth. The Lord Jesus Christ Himself called our attention to the safe Way:

Jesus said to him, "I am the way, the truth, and the life. No one comes to the Father except through Me. If you had known Me, you would have known My Father also; and from now on you know Him and have seen Him."
John 14:6-8 New King James Version (NKJV)

Jesus Christ is God's Road Map to Paradise in eternity. He is the one that directs and guide us to the right and safe route to heaven. The Broadway, which is the most popular route, takes travelers on it to the place of eternal divine punishment created and reserved for sinners. Fire. My dear reader, are you on the journey to eternity via the Broad Way or the Narrow Way? I want you to pause for a while and think seriously about the road on which you are traveling. At a point in your journey to eternity, you will get to a checkpoint which is the FIRST death. And when that happens, you have gotten to the point of no return.

Danger Ahead, Exit The Broadway Now!

Yes, now we know that eternity is an inevitable journey for everyone to embark upon. We also know that there are only two destination points in the journey to eternity. Also we now know that there are only two routes leading to these two destinations. It now behoves everyone traveling on the journey to eternity to ask the following questions:

(a) What is my destination?
(b) Which road am I travelling?

Yes, my dear reader, there are just two terminuses in the journey to eternity:

(a) Paradise in heaven
(b) Eternal life of torments in Hell, the place of eternal divine punishment created and reserved for sinners.

While on the journey to eternity, we will encounter many bus stops. Nevertheless, there is a well defined terminus for the journey irrespective of what happened within the space or time during the journey. For us as Christians, it is a journey expected to terminate in Paradise, the heavenly City prepared by God Himself for us. But for those who refused to believe in Jesus Christ and accept the work of redemption He did on the Cross, their destination is Hell, the place of eternal divine punishment created and reserved by God for sinners.

Just as we said earlier, there are two possible routes that will take you to the two possible destination points in eternity. The choice of your routes in regard to the journey into eternity must be carefully made. You need to be conscious of the implications of your choice of route and its consequences.

The way to Paradise has been made clear by Jesus Christ:

"I am the way, the truth, and the life. No one comes to the Father except through Me. If you had known Me, you would have known My Father also; and from now on you know Him and have seen Him."John 14:6-8 New King James Version (NKJV)

Today, if you are travelling on the Broadway, then you are not following the Divine Roadmap —Jesus Christ. You need to exit the Broadway now because serious danger lies ahead. And there is only ONE exit door from the Broad Way. And that only Door is Jesus Christ.

I am the door. If anyone enters by Me, he will be saved, and will go in and out and find pasture. 10 The thief does

**not come except to steal, and to
kill, and to destroy. I have
come that they may have life, and that they may
have it more abundantly.
John 10:9-10 New King James Version (NKJV)**

Unless you enter that Door (Jesus Christ), you will never make it to Paradise in Heaven, the destination God has chosen for you. How can you enter that Door? It is very simple. Just confess your sins and believe in the Lord Jesus Christ. Accept Him as your personal Lord and Saviour and you are home and dry! If you miss Christ, you will miss Heaven.

CHAPTER ELEVEN

LEARNING TO TRUST GOD IN A LIFELONG WALK WITH HIM

In chapter three, verse three, of the Book of Amos, the prophet asked a very critical question: "Can two walk together, except they be agreed?" Prophet Amos' question strikes at the core of the main issue involved in a relationship between two entities. For our own purpose here in this chapter, we are specifically talking about the relationship between a believer and God Almighty.

I believe there is no need to belabour the point the prophet is making in the above scripture. Indeed, it is an irrefutable fact that a meaningful rapport between two individuals is impossible without the two of them having an agreement. Any two people who are in a relationship, irrespective of the type of relationship they are engaged in, must have some things in common; they must trust each other and share some values that are dear to them. This same principle applies to the relationship between God and man. Our faith and trust in God are crucial for us to have a successful walk with Him. This point was made very clear by the writer of the Book of Hebrews in Chapter Eleven. Let's listen to him:

> **By faith Abel offered unto**
> **God a more excellent sacrifice**
> **than Cain, by which he obtained witness**

that he was righteous, God testifying of his gifts:
and by it he being dead yet speaketh. By faith Enoch
was translated that he should not see death; and was
not found, because God had translated him: for before
his translation he had this testimony,
that he pleased God.
But without faith it is impossible
to please him: for he that
cometh to God must believe that he is, and that he is
a rewarder of them that diligently seek him.
(Hebrew 11:4-6 KJV)

It is clear from the foregoing that there is no denying the fact
that an unshaken belief and trust in God's unlimited capacity
to meet all our needs, i.e., protection and daily provisions, as
well as helping us to overcome the challenges of life, are very
important for us to succeed in our daily walk with Him. Now,
before we go further, let's talk about what trust is. What is
trust?

What is trust?

Dictionary.com defines trust as "reliance on the integrity,
strength, ability, surety, etc., of a person or thing; confidence
or confident expectation of something" [1]In its definition of
trust, the Merriam-Webster.com Dictionary says trust is "to
place confidence; assured reliance on the character, ability,
strength, or truth of someone or something, or one in which
confidence is placed."[2]

According to the Oxford Dictionary, trust is "the belief that
somebody or something is good, sincere, honest, etc. and will

not try to harm or trick you". For Cambridge Dictionary, the word trust means "to <u>believe</u> that someone is good and <u>honest</u> and will not <u>harm</u> you, or that something is <u>safe</u> and reliable" [3]The dictionary explains further that trust is a "firm belief in the reliability, truth, or ability of someone or something[4].

Now, What Has Trust Got To Do With Relationship With God

Life is full of all kinds of challenges and trials. As we navigate the tortuous journey of life and the attendant challenges, only the power and mercy of God, through the blood of His precious Son, Jesus Christ, can see us through and help us help arrive at our desired destinations. We need the power of God to insulate us from the damaging consequences of trials and challenges that may come our way. In John chapter 16, the Lord Jesus Christ made us to know that, as children of God, we are not insulated from the challenges and trials of life. Let's listen to the Lord:

These things I have spoken to you, that
In me, you might have peace. In the world,
shall have tribulation, but be of good cheer; I
have overcome the world. (John 16:33)

to We can safely infer from our Lord's statement that challenins of life and difficult situations will surely arise in the course of carrying out our daily activities. However, we are not left without help. All we need to do is have a steady daily walk with God. We need t have Him by our side all the time. This is what we need to do to overcome life's trials and challenges. We need to walk daily with God and also to "place our <u>confidence</u> in Him. We must trust, <u>depend</u>, and totally rely on His immeasurable ability, strength, and power to secure and deliver us whenever trials of life come our way.

There is no doubting the limitless power of God and His ability to save His people whenever the storms of life arise. God is ever ready to stretch out His mighty hands to rescue us from perishing in the storm, as Jesus did when He rescued Peter from sinking while he was walking on the sea. Again, let's go to the Bible:

And in the fourth watch of
the night Jesus went unto them,
walking on the sea. And when the disciples
saw him walking on the sea, they were troubled,
saying, It is a spirit; and they cried out for fear. But
straightway Jesus spake unto them, saying, Be of good
cheer; it is I; be not afraid. And
Peter answered him and said,
Lord, if it be thou, bid me come
unto thee on the water. And
he said, Come. And when Peter
was come down out of the
ship, he walked on the water, to
go to Jesus. But when he
saw the wind boisterous, he was
afraid; and beginning to
sink, he cried, saying, Lord, save
me. And immediately
Jesus stretched forth his hand, and caught him, and
said unto him, O thou of little faith, wherefore
didst thou doubt? And when they were
come into the ship, the wind ceased.
Then they that were in the ship

**came and worshipped him,
saying, Of a truth thou art
the Son of God.
(Mathew 14:25–33 KJV)**

Just like Peter, I too have experienced this awesome power of Jesus to save His children from the storm in my many battles with the storms of life. One of these battles was when I was afflicted with a mysterious cancer ailment. However, by His grace, I miraculously survived the satanic attack, which originated from spiritual arrows of cancer and disease fired into my life in the dream. The spiritual arrows resulted in a severe, life-threatening high-level cancer, which doctors at Boston Cancer Medical Center concluded would take away my life. But by His grace, God saved me and healed me.

Prior to the attack, I never had any premonition that the night was going to be a night never to be forgotten in my life. Nothing foreboding occurred before I went to bed that could indicate that something sinister was lurking in my well-lit bedroom, to be unleashed by the devil against me later that night. As usual, I have had a very busy day at work, and I couldn't wait for the night to come so as to have some good rest. Indeed, the night was usually the time for me to reflect on what happened during the day and also to plan ahead for the following day. So, after a delicious meal and my night prayers, I went to my bedroom, expecting a blissful night's rest that my aching body was demanding. Unfortunately, that was not to be.

Soon after I lied on the bed, I slept off. Then, deep in the night, the enemy came. Satan used a woman to launch a debilitating attack against me. The Satanic missile was fired from home, in Benin City, in Edo State, Nigeria. Prior to that night, I had never been serious with God, even though I had been going to church. I was never a committed Christian, so they could easily get me. I was deep in sin. I was drinking alcohol, and my hobby was going after women, dating as many as came my way. I spurned every offer made to me by God to have a change of heart, begin to walk on the path of holiness and righteousness, and return to His plan for my life. I was a recalcitrant child in the hands of a loving and merciful God. This was the situation in which I was when the enemy struck deep in the hours of that night.

The woman came to me in the dream with a cup of coffee, and she asked me to drink it. I objected and told her that I don't drink coffee, and even if I want to drink coffee, I drink it in the morning, not at night, and now it's too late in the night to drink coffee. She insisted, forced my mouth open, and put the coffee in my mouth. Immediately I began to cough in the dream, and the cough became so serious that I coughed out of my sleep. When I woke up, I realized it was a satanic visitation.

In the Book of John, chapter fourteen, the Lord Jesus Christ declared:

Hereafter, I will not talk much with
You are the prince of this world.
cometh, and has nothing in me.
(John 14:30 KJV)

Yes, Satan came to Jesus Christ, but he couldn't find anything incriminating in the Lord. There was no sin in our Lord Jesus Christ's life. However, in my case, dear reader, when the Devil came that night, he found fornication, he found alcohol, he found many sinful things in me, and he added to my woes.

He gave me CANCER, which he packaged as a cup of coffee in the dream. In the morning, the cough that started in the dream continued unabated. I then decided to see my primary health physician in Boston, United States. After examining me, the doctor asked me to do an x-ray, a blood test, and some other tests. Later, he called me at home and told me that he had found some things in the reports of the tests I took and that he needed to refer me to a specialist. At that point in time, the coughing had escalated. So, without hesitation, I went to the specialist he asked me to see at Boston Medical Center. The specialist carried out another round of X-rays as well as many other medical examinations on me. At the end of the tests, the specialist told me that I had to undergo medical surgery. I told him that I did not think that my case, which was a mere cough, required surgery. I objected to his conclusion. The doctor looked at me straight in the face and declared:

"Your case isn't a mere cough! Let me be frank with you. From what I saw on the computer, if you do surgery, you will be alive for three months. If you refuse to do it, you will pass away in your sleep any moment from now".

The specialist further gave me a scary report that the cancer had eaten everything from my head down to my toe. The doctor's verdict shocked me to my bone marrow—that I had just three months to live! Then a thought quickly ran through my mind: I've just had a baby girl back home in Nigeria who I have not even seen! Does it mean I will never see this girl and I will just die like that? It then dawned on me that I must go through the operation because I don't want to die yet. So, I called my wife back home in Africa and told her, "Hey, I have been told to undergo an operation to deal with the sickness, so begin to pray for me".

I didn't survive the satanic cancer attack because I was holy. No, not at all. I survived by the mercy and grace God gave me to trust Him for the power to overcome the terrible trials of life.

I thank God for the grace He gave me to trust Him and defy and reject the reports of the doctors who gave me just three months to live. Instead, I trusted God and believed God's report. One of these critical reports from the doctors was the outcome of the several hours-long medical examinations carried out on me by medical cancer specialists.

During the medical examinations, they put their equipment on my chest. They went to my anus and put their equipment there. I opened my mouth, and they thrust something into my throat, and it went down to my chest to get what they needed from my chest. They carried out all kinds of examinations on me.

At the end of the examinations, which lasted several hours, the reports of the tests actually scandalized the medical personnel in the hospital. They said, based on their findings, that I was not supposed to be active and walk. I was supposed to be immobile, lying down on a spot, unable to move my legs! But here I was, not only moving around but also going to work! Then I told the doctor, "Doc, I am a Christian. It's true I can be afflicted, but I can't be that sick". The doctor retorted, "I have been the Chief Medical Doctor in this hospital for the past 35 years. I have seen several thousand Christians die in this hospital".

I concluded my conversation with the doctor by telling him that if other Christians have been dying in that hospital, I will not join them because I am different. He thereafter booked me for another operation appointment. But before I left the hospital, the doctor gave me some advice on the types of foods to eat and those I shouldn't eat, the kinds of drinks I can drink, and the ones to avoid, apparently to aid the proposed surgery. Then I left the hospital. I went through the surgery, which lasted seven solid hours. I survived it because of my trust in God. The almighty God is ever ready to save His children if only we can put our trust in Him and rest upon His assuring promises.

occasioned This is where many Christians are failing to trust God, which means believing in His reliability, His word, His ability, and His strength. The Bible says that God cannot lie. He always keeps his promises. He loves you and has good things in store for you.

What Does It Mean to Trust God? In Our Daily Walk With Him?

In the Book of Proverbs, chapter 3, verse 5, the Bible declares:

> **Trust in the Lord with
> all thine heart; and lean not
> unto thine own understanding.
> In all thy ways acknowledge him,
> and he shall direct thy paths.**
> (Proverbs 3:5-6 KJV)

As Christians, God expects us to put our trust in Him and rely on Him totally for all our needs. That is the message in the above scripture. As we walk daily with God, our heavenly Father wants us to have total confidence in Him. He wants us not to depend too much on our human knowledge, wisdom, and sometimes what science tells us, like the outcome of the medical investigations by doctors at Boston Cancer Medical Centre, who gave me only three months to put my house in order because science said I would surely die due to the high level of cancer infestation in my body.

It is rather unfortunate that many Christians in the present generation would rather lean on their own understanding and depend so much on human wisdom and counsel and their business or social connections to survive the challenges of life instead of relying totally on the fathomless power of their Creator. As the Bible says, if we are to overcome the ever-increasing economic, social, and political crises in our societies today, we need to acknowledge God in all our ways.

And if we are to acknowledge God in everything we do, all we need to do is simply trust His power and ability to guarantee our success in all our undertakings. Hence, we must commit everything we do to Him. If we do this, if we trust Him and look to Him for the success of all our endeavors, then life will be easier for us, and when trials come, we will not be shaken because He will be there for us to defend and protect us.

CHAPTER TWELVE

HOW TO TRUST GOD IN THE JOURNEY OF LIFE

In most cases, when challenges of life come, we believers in the present generation are often inclined to seek relief and solutions to our problems from our human knowledge and capacity rather than run to God for panacea to the problems.

In such circumstances, we often resort to trusting human knowledge, competence, and technology to overcome our challenges. And the consequences of such actions can be calamitous. Indeed, life experiences have shown that our failure to totally trust and rely on God to meet our daily needs and fight our battles for us often results in avoidable trouble. No wonder, Joseph Medlicott Scriven, the writer of the wonderful song **"What a Friend We Have in Jesus,"** lamented in one of the verses of the song the trouble we often bring on ourselves because we fail to avail ourselves of the opportunities available in Jesus to solve and overcome the challenges we face in the journey of life. The song goes thus:

**What a friend we have!
in Jesus, all our sins and griefs
to bear! What a privilege to carry
everything to God in prayer!
O what peace we often forfeit,
O what needless pain we bear—all**

**because we do not carry
everything to God in prayer!** [1]

The Lord, in Psalm 146, warned us about the futility of putting our trust in human knowledge and ability instead of God to solve our problems:

**Put not your trust in princes,
nor in the son of man, in whom there is no help.
His breath goeth forth; he returneth
to his earth; in that very
day, his thoughts perish. Happy is he that hath the
God of Jacob for his help, whose hope is in the Lord
his God: Which made heaven, and earth, the sea,
and all that therein is: which keepeth truth for ever;
which executes judgment for the oppressed; which
gives food to the hungry. The Lord looseth the
prisoners: The Lord opens the eyes of the blind; the
Lord raises them that are bowed down; the Lord loves
the righteous. The Lord preserveth the strangers;
he relieveth the fatherless and widow; but the way
of the wicked he turns upside down. The Lord shall
reign for ever, even your God, O Zion, unto all
generations. Praise the Lord! (Psalm 146:3–10 KJV)**

Again, the loving Father gave us a reminder in Psalm 125 about His availability and assurance that He will always stand by us in times of trouble, fight our battles for us, and meet our financial, social, and other needs if only we can put our trust in Him.

Let's hear the Lord speak through the Psalmist:

They who trust in the Lord shall
be like Mount Zion, which cannot be removed,
but abideth for ever. As the
mountains are round about
Jerusalem, so the Lord is round about his people
from henceforth, even for ever. For the rod of
the wicked shall not rest upon the lot of the
righteous; lest the righteous put forth their
hands unto iniquity. (Psalm 125:1–3 KJV)

In His sermon on the mountain, in Chapter six of the Book of Matthew, the Lord Jesus counseled us to totally trust and rely on God's inexhaustible provisions to meet our daily needs instead of putting our trust in our abilities, human knowledge, science, and 21st century technologies. Again, let's listen to our Lord:

Therefore, I say to you, Take no
thought for your life, what ye shall eat, or what ye
shall drink; nor yet for your body,
what ye shall put on. Is not
Is life more than meat, and the body more than
raiment? Behold the fowls of the air; for they sow not,
neither do they reap, nor gather into barns; yet your
heavenly Father feeds them. Are you not much better
than they are? Which of you, by taking some thought,
can add one cubit to his stature? And why take
your thoughts for granted? Consider the lilies of the
field and how they grow; they toil not, nor do they
spin. And yet I say unto you, That even Solomon,
in all his glory, was not arrayed like one of these.
Therefore, if God so clothes the grass of the field,
which today is, and tomorrow is cast into the oven,

127

shall he not much more clothe you, O ye of little
faith? Therefore, take no thought, saying, What shall
we eat? Or, What shall we drink? Or, wherewithal
shall we be clothed? (For after all these things do the
Gentiles seek, for your heavenly Father knows that
you have need of all these things.) But seek ye first
the kingdom of God and his righteousness, and all
these things shall be added unto you. Take therefore
no thought for the morrow; for the morrow shall
take thought for the things of itself. Sufficient to
the day is the evil thereof. (Matthew 6:25–34 KJV)

As our Lord Jesus pointed out in this sermon, we must put our
trust firmly in the ability of God to meet our needs because
He cares for us, as Apostle Peter told us:

Humble yourselves, therefore.
under the mighty hand of God, that he
may exalt you in due time: Casting all your
care upon him, for he careth for you.
1 Peter 5:6-7 KJV)

However, instead of putting our trust in the Lord and making
trust our watchword, whenever we are faced with the daunting
realities of life, we often substitute trust for fear when we are
overwhelmed by the problems. We allow anxieties and fear—
the fear of an unknown future that could be unfavorable—
to dominate and control our thoughts and emotions.
Consequently, we jettison trust in God, and we cling to our
options for solutions to our problems. In such a situation, our
thinking becomes clouded by worry, and our faith in God is
extinguished.

We Need the Help of the Holy Spirit to Trust God

Humanly speaking, it's not an easy thing to trust God when we are faced with very daunting situations. The decision to trust God when we are in dire situations is a strong choice we have to make, even when our thoughts, feelings, or circumstances are telling us otherwise. In such inauspicious circumstances, it's only the Holy Spirit that can help us put our trust in God for solutions to our problems. Apostle Paul, in his letter to early Christians, also made this point in the Book of Philippians when he declared, For it is God who works in you both to will and to do of his good pleasure" (Philippians 2:13 KJV).

Indeed, we need to know that putting our trust in God does not mean that we have to ignore the realities of the daunting situations facing us. What is required of us is to commit ourselves to a life of absolute faith and trust in God, just as Abraham did when God asked him to sacrifice his only son, Isaac, to him. Let's go to the Book of Genesis:

And Isaac spake unto Abraham his father, and said, My father: and he said, Here am I, my son. And he said, Behold the fire and the wood: but where is the lamb for a burnt offering? And Abraham said, My son, God will provide himself a lamb for a burnt offering: so they went both of them together. And they came to the place which God had told him of; and Abraham built an altar there, and laid the wood in order, and bound Isaac his son, and laid him on the altar upon the wood.

And Abraham stretched forth his hand, and took
the knife to slay his son. And the angel of the Lord
called unto him out of heaven, and said, Abraham,
Abraham: and he said, Here am I. And he said, Lay
not thine hand upon the lad, neither do thou any
thing unto him: for now I know that thou fearest
God, seeing thou hast not withheld thy son, thine
only son from me. And Abraham lifted up his eyes,
and looked, and behold behind him a ram caught in
a thicket by his horns: and Abraham went and took
the ram, and offered him up for a burnt offering
in the stead of his son. And Abraham called the
name of that place Jehovah jireh: as it is said to this
day, In the mount of the Lord it shall be seen.
(Genesis 22:7–14 KJV)

Steps to Trusting God

Joseph Medlicott Scriven, in his songs, lamented that we often
forfeit, a lot of peace and bear needless pain just because we
do not trust God enough to take all our challenges to Him,
who only has the capacity to solve all our problems because we
do not carry everything to God in prayer! [2] What Scriven
is saying in essence is that, because God loves us, we should
put our trust in Him by talking to Him about all our feelings
and circumstances through prayer. We should not allow the
emotions of fear and anxiety to dominate and rule our lives.
God is always willing to listen to us and help us.

Step One: Be An Avid Bible Reader

The Bible is the word of God. The Word of God is God Himself. In John Chapter 1, verse 1, the Bible says "In the beginning was the Word, and the Word was with God, and the Word was God".

If we must take God as a close friend whom we can and should trust, then we need to have an intimate relationship with Him. We need to know him. The only way to know God intimately is through His Word, the Bible. It is therefore important for us to go to where we can find Him—in the Bible. Hence, we need to become avid Bible readers so that we will be able to know God, whom we want to commit everything about our lives to. Even if it's a single chapter or only a few verses that we can read in a day, that will be a good beginning if we are consistent.

When we read the Bible regularly, we will see numerous of God's promises, which the Bible says are yea and amen. In the Bible, we shall find situations in which God fulfilled His promises as well as various stories about God's faithfulness to His people. When we see examples of God's good character in His word, our own faith will be strengthened because we'll see that God is the same yesterday, today, and forever.

It therefore follows that if God was faithful to His promises in the lives of the people in the Bible, we can rest assured that He will also be faithful in our own lives too. If God has never lied before, we can be assured He won't lie to us (see Number 23:19). God is incomparable with human beings. Human beings do change in character and behavior, but God does not. God is constant and unchanging in character. He is ever-reliable, immutable, and

We can trust God through constant Dialogue through Prayer

One of the best ways to have a sustainable relationship with a friend is to constantly engage in conversations or exchange ideas with a view to achieving certain objectives. Such interaction will help the relationship develop and become stronger. In relation to God, this same principle applies. It is therefore imperative for us to build and sustain our trust in God by engaging in conversations with Him. Such conversations occur through prayers. While we talk to God through prayers, He can respond to us in a myriad of ways, such as His Word in the Bible, the Holy Spirit, a fellow believer, and other means He can choose to respond to our prayers. to convey a message to us.

Sometimes God may not answer our prayers right away, or in the way we want, one thing we can be assured of is that delay in answering our prayers can never be denied.

[1] https://hymnary.org/text/what_a_friend_we_have_in_jesus

[2] https://hymnary.org/text/what_a_friend_we_have_in_jesus

CHAPTER THIRTEEN

WALKING THE TALK OF YOUR TRUST IN GOD

M any years ago, I got caught in heavy storms of life. In the eye of the raging storms were my business, my family, and my entire life. It became an existential issue as my existence came under debilitating spiritual attacks that resulted in the collapse of my businesses. Prior to that time, I had been involved in a very lucrative business deal with a banking and investment company here in the United States. The US-based company identified lots of existing business opportunities in Nigeria that we could exploit and earn good returns from.

And without much ado, I went into partnership with the company because, for me, it was a good business to invest in. We set up a team that was given the mandate to come to Nigeria and commence business operations. The company supported us with lots of money and everything we needed to operate successfully. When we got to Nigeria, we set up our operational base at Solanke Street, in Ajao Estate, in Oshodi/Isolo Local Government Area of Lagos State. Indeed, everything was going well for me. I had so many staff that helped me in marketing our goods, and at regular intervals, we were receiving containers of goods sent in from the US and Australia, and we were doing well in business.

However, all of a sudden, these storms of life came. Within a short while, everything that had been going well went awry.

As the storms continued to rage, a meltdown occurred in our operations, and the entire business collapsed. I lost so much to the storms, among which were 15 cars, three containers of goods that I couldn't claim from the wharf, and many other things. Above all, I lost my peace. I nearly died.

Nevertheless, in the midst of these raging storms, God gave me the grace to hold on to His anchor, which was my saving grace. I ran to Jesus, who indeed was my tower strength in the midst of the crises. I drew strength and courage from songs like Ruth Caye Jones' song, *In Times Like This:*

In times like these, you need a Savior.
In times like these, you need an anchor.
Be very sure. Your anchor holds and grips
the solid rock! This rock is Jesus. Yes, He's
the One. This rock is Jesus, the only one.
Be very sure. Your anchor holds and grips
the solid rock!

In times like these, you need the Bible. In times
like these, do not be idle. Be very sure. Your
anchor holds and grips the solid rock!

This rock is Jesus. Yes, He's the One.
This rock is Jesus, the only one. Be very
sure. Your anchor holds and grips the solid rock!

In times like these, I have a Savior.
In times like these, I have an anchor.
I'm very sure. My anchor holds and
grips the solid rock!
This rock is Jesus.

Yes, He's the One. This rock is Jesus,
the only one. Be very sure. Your anchor
holds and grips the solid rock! [1]

Yes, in the midst of the billowing storm, Jesus was my anchor. He saved me from the billowing waves of the storms. God helped me to hold on to my faith and trust in Him, and my anchor held on to the solid rock—Jesus Christ. Following the collapse of the business edifice I had built, I had to pack my bags and baggage and leave Nigeria. I went back to the US and started all over again from scratch.

Upon my return to the US, God, in His infinite mercy and grace, rescued me from the state of doldrums in which I was. I reorganized myself and became strong enough to go into another business. This time around, I went into the printing business. Alas, I never knew that the powers that were engineering the storms were still at work! They have not stopped the attacks against my life.

Nonetheless, driven by the desire to be back in business again, I got some very big printing machines in the US, and pronto, I took them to Nigeria. On getting to Nigeria, I established two printing presses in Benin City, in Edo State, Nigeria. Apart from the two printing presses, I also have a shop where we sell printing machine accessories as well as a gift shop. And beside my printing business, I also ventured into songwriting and music production. My intention then was to settle down in Nigeria and continue with the business. Things were indeed going well again for me after my disastrous experiences in the previous buying and selling business in Lagos. Fresh hope had arisen from the ruins of the previous business operations in Lagos.

But, all of a sudden, the storms made a return. This time around, they were more devastating! The crisis began with a car accident involving the music producer and a vocalist in my musical group. These two men were involved in a ghastly accident on their way from Lagos to Benin. They had gone to Lagos, the economic capital of Nigeria, to sell some of our machine parts, which we needed to dispose of. As a matter of fact, I was supposed to go on the journey to Lagos to sell the parts, but I later asked our music engineer to embark on the journey. Our vocalist also requested to join the music producer on the trip to Lagos, but I objected to his request. I wanted the producer to go alone. I never approved the vocalist's request to travel along with the music engineer. Nevertheless, the lead vocalist went with the music engineer, and on their way back from Lagos to Benin, they had a fatal accident. The vocalist died in the crash, while the music engineer was in a state of coma with a broken leg for more than a month. After regaining consciousness, the engineer had to stay in the hospital for close to nine (nine) months.

Amid the crisis, I arranged the burial of the vocalist while I was also picking up the bills of the engineer in the hospital. It was a terrible time in my life. However, again, Jesus, my solid rock was there for me. He strengthened my faith and trust in Him and helped me to hold on to His promises that I would surely overcome in spite of the billowing wave of the storm.

The family of the late vocalist made things very difficult for me. They accused me of killing their son and threatened to kill me and my family members in return for the death of their son. On several occasions, they planned to set our house ablaze whenever we were in the house and get us burned to death. Consequent upon the threat, we had to vacate our house and relocate to an uncompleted building, where we took refuge. In the midst of the raging storm, I give glory to God because He was always by our side as we walked through the fiery furnace of life.

> **When you pass through the waters,**
> **I will be with you, and through**
> **the rivers, they shall not**
> **Overflow thee: when thou walkest**
> **through the fire, thou shalt**
> **not be burned; neither shall the flame kindle**
> **upon you. For I am the Lord thy God, the Holy**
> **One of Israel, thy Saviour: I gave Egypt for**
> **thy ransom, Ethiopia, and Seba for you. Since**
> **thou wast precious in my sight, thou hast been**
> **honorable, and I have loved thee; therefore, I**
> **will give men for you and people for your life.**
> **Fear not, for I am with you. (Isaiah 43:2-5 KJV)**

Indeed, God never forsakes us. He helped us to anchor our trust and hope in Jesus Christ, His Son. The solid rock, Jesus Christ, was with us, even right inside the storms.

After we had gone through so much harassment, attacks, intimidation, and harrowing experiences, the father of the late vocalist later came around to confess that the boy's death was spiritually stage-managed. He owned up to the killing of his son through spiritual manipulation. The man's confession led to our eventual exoneration.

However, just as we were getting out of that calamitous experience, another tragedy struck again. It was another death that occurred in the precinct of my building. The incident occurred on one of our printing presses. A customer brought a job to the press. As the customer's job was being attended to, he sat in the waiting room waiting for his job to be done. He got himself a bottle of soft drink to refresh himself while waiting for his job. As he was drinking the soft drink he bought himself, he suddenly slumped and died instantly. While we were contending with the tragedy that occurred at the press, thieves went to the Gifts Shop and burgled it.

Again, as it occurred with the business operations at Ajao Estate in Lagos, which was shut down as a result of the storms, I had no choice other than to close down the printing businesses. My wife had to relocate to Lagos with two kids. We abandoned our comfortable accommodations in Benin City and had to squat with a friend in Lagos. Yet, the storm continued to rage against us in Lagos until the Lord quelled it.

Walking the Talk in the Midst of Storms

By the mercy and grace of God, my family and I survived all the storms that raged against us. Although we suffered heavy material losses, like Apostle Paul, who survived a heavy storm and the consequent shipwreck while being transported to Rome by his accusers, my family and I came out of the storms alive. In the midst of the storms, like Apostle Paul, we drew strength for survival from God's promises in the Bible, a series of prayers, and fervent faith and trust in the power of God to save to the uttermost. Although it wasn't easy, God helped us to walk the talk of our faith and keep trusting Him. As believers, our trust and faith in God must be activated and given expression, no matter how difficult the situation may be. In the course of our daily walk with God, challenges of life will surely arise in several areas of our lives, as Jesus Christ has warned us in the book of John:

These things I have spoken to you, that
In me, you might have peace. In the world,
shall have tribulation, but be of good cheer; I
have overcome the world. (John 16:33 KJV)

As beloved children of God, we must take into cognizance the fact that God is always ready to order every step we take in the course of walking with Him daily if only we can totally rely on Him. There is no doubting the fact that sometimes things may not go the way we want them to. This is the point that the Lord Jesus Christ made in John 16:33. Jesus warned us and called our attention to the fact that being children of God who have faith in Him will not prevent the storms of life from coming. They will come, but whenever they come, Jesus said He will be by our side as we battle with the storms.

It is rather unfortunate that some Christians have been given the impression that once they accept Jesus Christ as their Lord and Savior, all their problems will be solved. No, that is not true. Believing in Jesus Christ does not exclude us from the problems of life. Only those who are dead and buried six feet below, in the ground, are problem-free.

The truth of the matter is that no matter what we do, whether we believe in God or not, the problems of life will always exist. As believers in the Lord Jesus Christ, our saving grace is the assurance the Savior has already given us: "**But be of good cheer; I have overcome the world. (John 16:33)**. Yes, the problems are there, but they are nothing for us to fear because our Savior and Defender are always by our side. Therefore, we can be confident that our God is up to the task of solving any problem of life that the Devil may sponsor against us.

As we learn day-by-day to apply our faith and trust in God in our daily walk with Him, our confidence in His ability and power to fight our battles for us, as well as His ability to help us meet our needs at the various points where we need Him, will continue to grow and increase. We shall then realize that in any situation in which we may find ourselves, God is always by our side, helping us to navigate through the difficult situations. He will surely give us the required grace, courage, and strength to survive the difficulties, pains, and fears.

No matter the situation in which we find ourselves, we must not be overwhelmed by the storms of life. We must endeavor to walk the talk of our professed faith and trust in God through clear demonstrations of our trust in Him by holding the forte amidst the raging storms of life because Jesus is ever near us and He won't abandon us.

[1]https://namethathymn.com/christian-hymns/in-times-like-these-lyrics.html

CHAPTER FOURTEEN

ABRAHAM, LIKE ENOCH, ALSO WALKED THE TALK

A braham is reputed to be the Father of Faith. We read in several chapters of the Book of Genesis how the father of faith walked the talk of his faith in God. Abraham was able to walk with God because of his unwavering faith and trust in God. Abraham believed in God, trusted him, and acted upon the promises he received from God even when nothing had happened. Abraham believed that God would do what He had said He would do, and without being prompted, he acted on the basis of those promises.

In Genesis Chapter 12, Abraham, who was already in his old age and also childless, got a wonderful promise from God. God promised to give him a child through whom Abraham would become a big nation. Yet, at the time the promise was given, Abraham was already a 75-year-old man. Let's go to the Bible:

Now the Lord had said to Abram, Get thee out of thy country, and from thy kindred, and from thy father's house, unto a land that I will shew thee: And I will make of thee a great nation, and I will bless thee, and make thy name great; and thou shalt be a blessing; and I will bless them that bless thee, and curse him that curseth thee; and in thee shall all families of the earth be blessed. And Abram passed through the land unto the place of Sichem, unto the plain of Moreh.

And the Canaanite was then in the land. And the Lord appeared unto Abram and said, Unto thy seed will I give this land, and there built he an altar unto the Lord, who appeared unto him. (Genesis 12:1–4, 7–6KJV)

In spite of all these promises that God made to Abraham, Sarah, his wife, remained barren, and Abraham had no child many years after these promises were made. In chapter 13, the Almighty God not only reiterated his promise of an offspring to Abraham but also promised to give him the whole of the land where he dwelled.

And the Lord said unto Abram, after
that Lot was separated from him, lift up
now thine eyes, and Look from the place
where thou art northward, southward, eastward,
and westward: For all the land which thou seest, to
thee will I give it, and to thy seed for ever. And I will
make thy seed as the dust of the
earth, so that if a man
can number the dust of the earth,
then shall thy seed also
be numbered. Arise, walk through
the land in the length
of it and in the breadth of it; for
I will give it unto you.
(Genesis 13:14–17 KJV)

As we moved on in the book of Genesis, we realized that by Genesis 15, Father Abraham, who was probably by then 85 years old, was still childless, yet he remained unperturbed. He held on to his faith and trust in God. And having been impressed by Abraham's faith in Him, God renewed His promise to

Abraham, this time around with an oath, because Abraham has walked the talk of his faith and trust in God.

> **After these things, the word of the Lord**
> **came unto Abram in a vision,**
> **saying, Fear not, Abram:**
> **I am your shield and your exceedingly great reward.**
> **And Abram said, Lord God, what will thou give**
> **me, seeing I go childless, and the steward of my**
> **house is this Eliezer of Damascus? And Abram said,**
> **Behold, to me thou hast given no seed; and, lo, one**
> **born in my house is mine heir. And, behold, the**
> **word of the Lord came unto him, saying, This shall**
> **not be thine heir; but he that shall come forth**
> **Out of thine own bowels shall be thine heir. And**
> **he brought him forth abroad and said, Look now**
> **toward heaven, and tell the stars, if thou be able to**
> **number them; and he said unto him, So shall thy**
> **seed be. And he believed in the Lord, and he counted**
> **it to him for righteousness. (Genesis 15:1–6 KJV)**

Indeed, God's promise of an offspring for Abraham wasn't fulfilled until 25 years after the promise was given, as we read in Genesis chapter 21.

> **And the Lord visited Sarah as he had said,**
> **and the Lord did unto Sarah as**
> **he had spoken. For Sarah**
> **conceived and bore Abraham a son in his old age at**
> **the set time of which God had spoken to him. And**
> **Abraham called the name of his son that was born**
> **unto him, whom Sarah bore to him, Isaac. And**
> **Abraham circumcised his son Isaac, who was eight**

days old, as God had commanded him. And Abraham was a hundred years old when his son Isaac was born to him. And Sarah said, God has made me laugh, so that all who hear will laugh with me. And she said, Who would have said unto Abraham that Sarah should have given children suckers? for I have born him a son in his old age. And the child grew and was weaned, and Abraham made a great feast the same day that Isaac was weaned (Genesis 21:1–8KJV).

Can We Emulate Abraham?

Dearly beloved, there is so much for us to learn from Abraham regarding how he walked the talk of his faith and trust in God. As believers living in the end-time era, the question we should ask ourselves is: "Are we ready to walk the talk of our trust in God as Abraham did? Are we ready to exercise the patience that Abraham exhibited in his walk with God? Do we have the spiritual character to keep trusting and believing the word of God even when nothing is happening concerning the promises He has made to us, either through His word in the Bible or promises made to us in our dreams or visions? The challenge facing Christians living in the present generation is how to successfully emulate Abraham.

We need to pray to God to give us the grace and power to live and walk with God the way Abraham did. Abraham did not only profess his faith and trust in God; he acted on the basis of his faith in God. He trusted what God had told him; he actually believed and acted on the promise God made to him that he would indeed have a multitude of descendants, even though he didn't have a child.

**And God said unto Abraham, As
For Sarai, thy wife, thou shalt not call her Sarai, but
Sarah, shall her name be? And I will bless her,
and give thee a son also of her; yea, I will bless
her, and she shall be a mother of nations; kings of
people shall be of her. Then Abraham fell upon
his face, laughed, and said in his heart, Shall a
child be born unto him that is a hundred years
old? And shall Sarah, who is ninety years old,
bear? (Genesis 17:15–17KJV).**

Abraham's absolute trust and faith are what he expects us to
have as believers. God wants us to trust what He has said, act
on His word, and live it out, even though, humanly speaking,
it may make no sense. We also saw the demonstration of this
absolute faith and trust in God by Noah. Noah believed God
that a deluge would actually come to sweep away the first world,
as God promised. Hence, Noah built an ark as instructed by
God in order to save himself and his family from the impending
flood that wiped away the obdurate people of the first world.

Other Patriarchs Too Walked
the Talk Of Their Faith

It is important in our daily walk with God to always remember
that some people who were flesh and blood like us—they were
not angels but human beings—have done what God is now
asking us to do. Yes, the Bible recorded that Enoch, Noah,
Abraham, Isaac, and Jacob, just to mention a few, also walked
the talk of their faith and trust in God.

They all trusted God and walked successfully with Him. You may say that it is easier said than done, and yes, you may be right to some extent. However, the truth is, if we too exercise or activate our faith in God, just as Enoch, Noah, Abraham, Isaac Jacob, and many others did, through God's grace, the Almighty God is ever-willing and ready to empower us with grace to do similar things that these patriarchs did in their lifetime.

When our trust and faith in God are activated, we will begin to easily trust and rely on God to meet all our needs. He will then become our rock and tower of strength, who will always help us overcome any challenge that may come our way.

What we need to do, like the aforementioned patriarchs, is to begin to have faith in God and also trust Him absolutely. We must begin to have unwavering faith and trust in God, believing that come rain or shine, God will do what He said He would do.

Enoch, Noah, Abraham, Isaac, and Jacob—all of them knew the power and immeasurable ability of God. They experienced it. They also knew that if they totally relied on Him, He would save and protect them. Hence, they put all their trust in him. It is little wonder that they experienced the mighty power of God in various areas of their lives when they needed Him. They were able to walk with him all through their lives.

Requirements for Walking the Talk of Your Faith and Trust in God

At this stage in our conversation, we can deduce from the foregoing that there are some indispensable virtues a person who wants to walk successfully with God and be the Enoch of our generation must possess.

Among these qualities are:

1. Absolute faith in God
2. Absolute Trust in God
3. Obedience to God's laws and commandments.
4. High level of endurance in times of adversity

The above are the qualities that we believers in today's world need to have to be able to successfully walk the talk of our avowed faith and trust in God. We need an uncompromising faith in God. We need the faith that will help us accept and believe all His promises and consequently act on them. We must totally rely on God, as the Book of Proverbs counseled us; we must not trust our own judgment or lean on our understanding but rather put our trust in God.

Trust in the Lord with all thine heart; and lean not unto thine own understanding. In all thy ways acknowledge him, and he shall direct thy paths. (Proverbs 3:5–6 KJV)

We must always remember that God is our heavenly Father, and He loves us and wants the best for us. He will never lead us astray or give us anything that is not good for us. By trusting

God and not our emotions and knowledge, we can build up our faith and trust in Him. Through faith, prayer, and obedience to God's commandments, we can experience His perfect love and guidance in every area of our lives. Enoch had unwavering faith and trust in God. This enabled him to have a close relationship with the Almighty, and eventually, the Bible told us that he was taken to heaven. He never experienced death. As believers, we are expected to walk with God in the same fashion as Enoch did.

Trust in God Begins With Our Faith in Him

**But without faith it is impossible
to please him: for he that cometh to
God must believe that he is, and that
he is a rewarder of them that diligently
seek him.(Hebrews 11:6 KJV)**

Faith is an important building block in developing a relationship with God. Without faith in God, we cannot please Him, as the Bible says. Hence, walking the talk of our faith and trust begins with having an uncompromising faith in God. Faith in God precedes our trust in Him. When you have faith or confidence in a person, you will necessarily develop trust in him or her. In the same way, we need to have faith in God and believe that He is able to meet all our needs and solve all our problems, no matter how difficult they are. We must also be obedient to His Word and humbly accept His will. It is only by doing so that we can experience the same level of relationship that Enoch and other patriarchs had with God.

Enoch walked the talk of his avowed faith and trust in God through obedience to God's laws and commandments. Enoch was able to walk successfully with God because he feared God and obeyed His laws. Enoch demonstrated his trust and faith in God through his intimate communion with Him and unalloyed loyalty and obedience to His will. Enoch totally leaned on God instead of his own ability and knowledge, as the Bible counseled us in the Book of Proverbs.

We Must Put Our Faith And Trust Into Action

Most of us believe in the power of God thanks to our personal experiences and through reading the Bible. But putting these beliefs into action can be a challenge for many children of God in today's world. Placing our trust in God is our choice, and one that we must make wholeheartedly. Unfortunately, in this area, not many believers today can confidently say they are doing well. Nevertheless, it is important for us as believers not only to trust God but to also put our trust and faith into action. We must also trust God, like the patriarchs did. We should believe that He will not fail us and won't let us down. If we as believers can believe that heaven and earth were created by God and that He controls all the powers—physical and spiritual—and all the resources in this world, then why should it be difficult for us to believe and trust God? Why can't we believe that He is able to meet all our needs, whereas the Bible told us that "The one who calls you is faithful, and He will do it?" (1 Thessalonians 5:24).

The grace to have unwavering trust in God and also put our faith and trust in God, the Lord will give us in Jesus' name. amen.

Printed in the United States
by Baker & Taylor Publisher Services